Therapeutic Engagement of Children and Adolescents

Play, Symbol, Drawing, and Storytelling Strategies

David A. Crenshaw

JASON ARONSON
Lanham · Boulder · New York · Plymouth, UK

Published in the United States of America
by Jason Aronson
An imprint of Rowman & Littlefield Publishers, Inc.

A wholly owned subsidiary of
The Rowman & Littlefield Publishing Group, Inc.
4501 Forbes Boulevard, Suite 200, Lanham, Maryland 20706
www.rowmanlittlefield.com

Estover Road
Plymouth PL6 7PY
United Kingdom

British Library Cataloguing in Publication Information Available

Library of Congress Cataloging-in-Publication Data

Crenshaw, David A.
  Therapeutic engagement of children and adolescents : play, symbol, drawing, and
storytelling strategies / David A. Crenshaw.
     p. ; cm.
  "A Jason Aronson book."
  Includes bibliographical references and index.
  ISBN-13: 978-0-7657-0570-9 (cloth : alk. paper)
  ISBN-10: 0-7657-0570-2 (cloth : alk. paper)
  ISBN-13: 978-0-7657-0571-6 (pbk. : alk. paper)
  ISBN-10: 0-7657-0571-0 (pbk. : alk. paper)
  1. Child psychotherapy. 2. Adolescent psychotherapy. 3. Therapeutic
alliance. 4. Psychotherapist and patient. I. Title. [DNLM: 1. Child. 2. Psychotherapy—
methods. 3. Adolescent. 4. Professional-Patient Relations. 5. Psychotherapeutic
Processes. WS 350.2 C915t 2008]
  RJ504.C75 2008
  618.92'8914--dc22

                                                                            2007042707

Printed in the United States of America

⊗™ The paper used in this publication meets the minimum requirements of
American National Standard for Information Sciences—Permanence of Paper
for Printed Library Materials, ANSI/NISO Z39.48-1992.

DEDICATION

Olga Silverstein

Olga Silverstein is a beloved, gifted, and innovative family therapist and a teacher beyond compare. Her wisdom and compassion have informed and inspired my work and multiple generations of family therapists who were privileged to take her courses, or workshops, or be supervised by her at the Ackerman Institute for the Family, where she is presently Faculty Emeritus. Olga is a master of therapeutic questioning, particularly relational questions, and I acknowledge a huge debt to her in influencing the development of the relational questions found in this book. She is also unsurpassed in her ability to explore the change/stability balance in families and to make explicit the negative consequences of change, so that the family can make an informed choice. What a rich legacy her career has left the field of family therapy; what a gift to all of us who were privileged to learn from her. Olga's refreshing directness, clinical incisiveness, verbal facility, knowledge of families, and finely honed family therapy skills put her in a class of her own. If only there were more like her.

Contents

1   Engaging Reluctant Children in Therapy   1
2   Relational Strategies to Engage Heart and Mind   7
3   The Therapeutic Use of Symbols to Engage Children and Adolescents   29
4   Building the Therapeutic Alliance by Honoring Strengths   45
5   Strategies to Strengthen the Self-Observer   57
6   Facilitating Empathy for Self and Others   83
7   Strategies to Access the Pain of Social Rejection   99
8   Strategies to Address Grief and Traumatic Loss   117
9   The "Quest for Home" Strategies   131
10   The Delicate Therapeutic Operation of Facilitating Hope   145

References   159
Index   167

• 1 •

Engaging Reluctant Children in Therapy

Overview: Psychotherapy at its best is part science and part art, and I hope it always remains so. Science and empirical research inform and guide clinical practice but when the child, teen, or family enters the office or therapy room, what takes place is a unique human encounter that is as much art as science. One of the crucial tasks in the therapy process is engagement. When children show up for therapy the therapist is faced with the challenge of engaging what are typically reluctant participants. For ease of communication, "child" or "children" will be used in this book to refer to both younger children and adolescents unless specifically stated otherwise.

Children typically are brought to therapy because someone else—usually a parent, a teacher, a school official, or a judge—has decided it would be a good idea for them to get therapy. The children are usually not sold on this idea. Middle-school children and teens are particularly not convinced of the virtues of going to therapy. Pre-teens are well-known for viewing the idea of going to talk to someone about personal problems as alien, if not complete madness. The therapist, upon arrival of such newcomers, is faced with the challenge to engage reluctant participants in the therapy process. This book is focused on helping child and adolescent therapists meet that challenge.

Upon entering the therapist's office, pre-teens and adolescents fear that the therapist immediately sees right through them; all their vulnerabilities exposed to this stranger in this baffling process called therapy. They don't understand at this initial point that therapy is a collaborative process; they expect that the therapist will use psychic X-ray powers to unmask them almost immediately. Others, because of the coercion used to round them up and herd them into the therapist's corral, view the whole process akin to being sent to the principal's office or standing before the judge and can't wait to get the punishment over and the sentence served. Still others might see some possible value to talking to a trained professional about issues they are struggling with but are mortified about the chance that they might be seen by friends coming in or out of the therapist's office and thereby branded "a psycho" by their peers. While stigma and shame associated with seeing a therapist has diminished over recent decades, it is still a factor for some young people.

Engaging children in psychotherapy typically requires a more proactive and directive approach than is typical in adult therapy. A positive and hopeful attitude, emphasizing the strengths of children, and expressing confidence in the therapy process are essential ingredients (Oetzel and Scherer, 2003; Rubenstein, 1996). The play, storytelling, drawing, and symbol strategies described in subsequent chapters offer youthful clients from preschool through adolescence a meaningful, engaging, and (especially for teens) a face-saving way to participate in therapy. Two decades of empirical research have consistently linked the quality of the alliance between therapist and client with therapy outcome (Horvath, 2001). Furthermore, Horvath explained that the magnitude of this relation appears to be independent of the type of therapy and whether the outcome is assessed from the perspective of the therapist, client, or observer.

The strategies should not be used as a "cookbook approach" to therapy nor do they represent a stand-alone approach to therapy. But they have in common the theme of focusing therapy on the important relationships in the child's life. They can be integrated into a wide range of therapy approaches and are especially compatible with theoretical orientations that give emphasis to interpersonal, social, and cultural determinants of personality. Relational Therapy is the orientation that I most closely identify with at this late point in my career, although I still view myself as Integrative in both theory and therapy rather than wedded to any one approach. Among the theories that emphasize relational factors are Relational Theory (DeYoung, 2003); Relational-Cultural Theory (Miller, 1986; Miller and Stiver, 1997); Relational Psychoanalysis (Mitchell and Aaron, 1999); Culturalist Psychoanalysis (Bonime, 1989); Family Systems Theory (Minuchin & Fishman, 1981; Minuchin and Nichols, 1993); Attachment Theory (Bowlby, 1980); and Interpersonal Neurobiological Theory (Schore 1994, 2003a, 2003b; Siegel 1999, 2007). Magnavita (2006) observes, "The relational matrix is the ultimate unifying principle of human development and of psychotherapy. It plays a central role in shaping and influencing human function and dysfunction" (p. 887).

Since more than two thousand studies (Kazdin, 2005) point to the crucial role of the therapeutic alliance in psychotherapy outcome research, these strategies offer a potentially valuable tool to strengthen the therapeutic alliance. It should be noted that the therapeutic relationship has not been shown to play a causal role in symptom/problem improvement. But the importance of this ingredient in the therapeutic equation is underlined by Kazdin's summarization that a vast number of research studies have shown that alliance or relationship processes early in treatment predicts (statistically) treatment outcome among adults. In fact, Kazdin observed, the better the alliance/relationship, the greater the change.

My aim is be jargon-free; a skill that the late Walter Bonime (1989), with whom I studied for over a decade, taught and advocated among his psychoanalytic colleagues. In fact, Bonime (1989) with his wife, Florence, who was a writer, penned an essay on "Psychoanalytic Writing: An Essay on Communication," in which he urged analytic writing that translates easily into "common speech." Unfortunately, much of contemporary psychoanalytic theory is shrouded in mystifying jargon.

There is no "one size fits all" path to healing. The theoretical orientations and therapy approaches outlined in the above paragraphs do not represent a comprehensive or exhaustive list of all the possible healing approaches, but they encompass frameworks broad enough in scope to take into account both the internal life of the child along with the social, familial, and cultural context in which the child's development takes place and they emphasize respect for the strengths of the child and family that I regard as essential.

PRACTICAL THERAPEUTIC STRATEGIES

Symbolic Play, Storytelling, Drawing, and Use of Symbols

This book details a range of specific strategies consisting of symbolic play, use of symbols, storytelling, and drawing to engage and touch the hearts and minds of children. An expanding body of empirical research demonstrates that—particularly with adolescents—providing some degree of choice with respect to their participation in therapy enhances the potential for therapeutic engagement (Church, 1994; Hanna and Hunt, 1999; Liddle, 1995; Loar, 2001; Oetzel and Scherer, 2003; Rubenstein, 1996). Oetzel and Scherer (2003) stated, "Engaging adolescents in psychotherapy and establishing a strong therapeutic alliance with adolescents require that therapists express empathy and genuineness, utilize developmentally appropriate interventions, address the stigma, and increase choice in therapy" (p. 215). The strategies can also be incorporated into a range of therapy modalities such as individual, group, and family therapy, as well as art therapy. I have applied the strategies exclusively in individual and family therapy but colleagues who do group therapy and art therapy report that they have found some of the strategies previously described (Crenshaw, 2004; 2006b) clinically useful within those modalities and I hope that will also be true of the ones described herein.

The strategies in this book are designed with the dual purpose of engaging children in the therapeutic process in a meaningful way and of strengthening the therapeutic alliance. As the therapeutic alliance is developed, children will be encouraged to share more about what really matters to them so that the therapy is more likely to touch the painful parts of the heart that need healing. Consistent with a Relational Therapy framework, many of the strategies contain a specific relational component to focus children in therapy on important connections and disconnections in their social world. The strategies of engagement are offered as examples of many potential others that are limited only by the imagination and creativity of the therapist. No claim is made that the strategies described are unusually innovative. I hope that sharing these specific interventions in detail will stimulate the creation of other such techniques that will be useful in engaging children in therapy.

Young children use talk, the language of words, to tell their stories when they no longer need play, the language of symbols. The strategies are designed for children who have passed the point where they comfortably and naturally engage in symbolic play. When some children reach age six or seven and older they will be able to engage in a verbal expressive therapy exchange without further need for fantasy play. The strategies in this book are intended for children who are not ready for verbal exchange as a primary means of communication in therapy but are too embarrassed to engage in play. Still other children, when they reach seven or older, will be able to deal with some topics directly in verbal exchange with the therapist but with other affectively charged issues will need the symbolic haven offered by symbolic play, drawings, storytelling, or symbol work to express themselves freely.

While some of the drawing strategies will overlap with methods of art therapy, I do not use drawings for diagnostic purposes. Those readers interested in drawings for diagnostic or interpretative purposes may consult the writings of Furth (2002), Klorer (2000), and Malchiodi (1998, 2003). The use of drawings and storytelling in psychotherapy with children and families enjoys a long tradition and a review of that literature is available (Crenshaw, 2006b) for interested readers and won't be repeated here.

Clinical Considerations and Cautions

Evocative strategies such as the ones in this book should only be used in the *Invitational Track* of child therapy as described in the Play Therapy Decision Grid (Crenshaw and Mordock, 2005a, pp. 62–78). Readers are urged to review carefully the clinical criteria for determining whether a child more appropriately belongs in the *Coping Track* (psychoeducational) or the *Invitational Track* (gradual confrontation of painful or traumatic events). The coping track (psychoeducational approach) is the place to start with children. The coping approach focuses on their strengths, building defense, and teaching social and problem solving skills before it moves into the more threatening territory of the invitational track. In the invitational track, the child is invited to go as far as possible in approaching the hurt. To use strategies like "Heartfelt Feelings" (Chapter 2) a therapist needs to have established a strong therapeutic alliance, ascertained that the child has sufficient ego resources to contain the anxiety generated by such direct focus on emotional experiences and a clear rationale as to why it could benefit the particular child in therapy.

One important way to assess the internal strengths of children to cope with anxiety is to monitor closely within sessions the level of tension in the child when certain topics are addressed. If the child can't focus, or wants to run out of the room, or withdraws to an unusual degree, clearly the anxiety around those particular topics is breaking through and disruptive to the child's functioning. This would be a sign that the child needs more work in the coping track and should not be encouraged to approach directly the painful or traumatic material until he or she shows the ability to cope with and contain the anxiety.

It is also important to inquire about the child's reactions following the session. If the child is disruptive in school or home following a session, it may be a sign of "spillover," which indicates that the child is overwhelmed by anxiety generated by therapeutic work in session. This would suggest the need for more work in the coping track.

These strategies are contraindicated in children who do not meet the criteria above and with children who do not need facilitation of their affective expression. They are especially contraindicated with children who have poor emotional control and are emoting in a chaotic, disorganized manner. If children become anxious while doing the strategies, the therapist should honor and respect their need to withdraw from participation. Doing so will convey to the child that the therapist is committed to making therapy a safe place.

In using potentially evocative techniques with children in therapy it is a guiding principle that the therapist must be careful to ensure that any activation of powerful emotions is something the therapist is prepared to handle. The Decision Grid for Play and Child Therapy (Crenshaw and Mordock, 2005a, 2005b) was developed precisely for this reason to guide the child therapist in making judgments about the child's readiness to approach emotionally laden material. Sometimes inexperienced child therapists push too hard because of their need to prove they are doing "good therapy." By proceeding patiently and respecting the pace the child needs to go, they may feel they are "not doing enough." This is a countertransference issue that contaminates the direction of the therapy. The therapy then becomes driven not by the child's needs but by the therapist's needs to prove adequacy. Child therapy should be child responsive, not determined by the needs of the therapist to validate competence nor driven by misplaced loyalty to a particular theoretical approach or technique.

Therapists should be familiar with a wide range of theoretical approaches and a comprehensive repertoire of interventions so they can call on what is needed at a particular time with a specific child in a particular situation and context.

Clinical judgment is needed to time the introduction of these strategies to a given child, and there is no substitute for the therapist's knowledge of the strengths and vulnerabilities of the individual child.

It is critical that readers never mistake the tools offered for the therapy itself. The therapeutic relationship is of overriding importance and the strategies are secondary to the healing role of the therapeutic alliance. The overriding goal of the various symbol, drawing, and storytelling strategies is to create portals of entry to the inner world of the child whether the work takes place in individual, group, or family therapy and to engage the child in a heartfelt therapeutic dialogue about his or her attachments that leads to increased understanding, acceptance, empathy for self and others, and a renewed sense of hope, based not on the strength of the therapist but on the child's and family's resources. It is the heartfelt relational, collaborative process of healing a hurt child.

· 2 ·

Relational Strategies to Engage Heart and Mind

*Ov*erview: *The strategies in this chapter, the Heartfelt Feelings Strategies (HFS) and the Heartfelt Feelings Coloring Card Strategies (HFCCS) are designed to facilitate exchanges in therapy with children regarding heartfelt emotions and key relationships. The strategies integrate cognitive and emotionally focused approaches in order to engage both the minds and hearts of children in a meaningful way. The cognitive tools are reflected in the follow-up questions to the "Heartfelt Feelings" strategies. These follow-up questions lead to further inquiries and dialogue that can incorporate the cognitive strategies of logical questioning, challenge and disputation of negative and pessimistic belief systems, and introduction of alternative perspectives. Emotionally focused strategies are evocative and intended to engage the heart and elicit the emotional life of the child. An approach that does not engage both is unlikely to have the same therapeutic impact.*

"THE HEARTFELT FEELINGS STRATEGIES" (HFS) (CHILDREN AGES 9 TO 17)

Purpose: *The HFS offers a series of activities to appeal to children that create opportunities for children to work on the key components of affect regulation: (1) identification of feelings; (2) labeling of feelings; and (3) verbal expression of feelings in a context-appropriate way; and also (4) to explore heartfelt emotions in relation to important people in their family and interpersonal world.*

Background and Rationale for the Heartfelt Feelings Strategies (HFS)

The "Heartfelt Feelings Strategies" (Crenshaw, 2006c) and the "Heartfelt Feelings Coloring Card Strategies" (Crenshaw, 2007a) are techniques that

7

can be used in play therapy, child therapy, family therapy, group therapy, and creative arts therapy to facilitate the child's expression of heartfelt emotions. Research has shown that verbal mediation skills play a critical role in modulating aggressive impulses in children (Burke, Crenshaw, Green, Schlosser, and Strocchia-Rivera, 1989). Young children typically lack a vocabulary to express their emotions and this strategy builds on others in the play therapy, child therapy, and art therapy literature such as the "Feelings Map" (Drewes, 2001)—sometimes called the "Gingerbread Person" or "Color-Your-Feelings" technique (Gil, 2006), the "Fun With Feelings" workbook (Land, 2000), and the Color-Your-Life technique (O'Connor, 1983) that offer children practical tools to expand their feelings vocabulary.

Many clinicians have used some variation of the heart shape in child play, art, and other creative arts therapies. Scott Riviere (2005) developed a technique that he called "Heart Felt Feelings" in his work with adolescents. Goodyear-Brown (2002) and H. Kaduson (personal communication, April, 2006) have created similar strategies for children. Riviere (2005) described his approach as similar to the one I developed for younger children. A difference between my use of the "Heartfelt Feelings Strategy" (HFS) and Riviere's use of the "Heart Felt Feelings" technique is that he uses the heart shape as a modification of the "Color-Your-Life" technique (O'Connor, 1983). Goodyear-Brown also uses her strategy in this way. Riviere explained that after adolescents pick a color for each emotion, the teens are then asked to color the amount of each feeling they have in their heart using the selected color. While pre-teens and adolescents are capable of dealing with proportion and the abstract concept of coloring the heart according to how much feeling in a generic sense they have in their heart, younger children usually find it difficult to comply with such abstract task requirements. There are always exceptions, but with school-age children, I find they handle this task more productively when they are given more structure. They might be asked, for example, to color in the heart according to how they felt when they were not invited to a friend's birthday party. Kaduson also structures her version of this technique in a similar way. This strategy works best for children nine and older, but some younger children, particularly if they are developmentally precocious, will be able to make productive use of this tool as well.

Aggressive and traumatized children experience emotions in an all-or-none manner (James, 1989). They benefit from learning there are different grades of intensity of feelings. A child need not be enraged or feel nothing at all. In between, children may experience irritation, annoyance, and anger but they don't usually know how to express these gradations of emotion. Learning the language of feelings is an important step in the process of developing emotional regulation skills. Finally, depicting their emotions in an artistic realm allows for symbolization of the raw emotions contributing to modulation and understanding by allowing new perspectives on the emotional experiences.

But the part of the HFS that most distinguishes it from all the similar strategies using the heart shape in child and family therapy as well as art therapy is that in both the "Heartfelt Feelings Strategy" and the "Heartfelt Feelings Coloring Card Strategy," (HFCCS) described later in this chapter, I emphasize two core domains: *Expressive* and *Relational.* The expressive component offers structured therapeutic practice in identifying, labeling, and expressing feelings. These are key skills in affect regulation and for developing social competence. Allan Schore (1994, 2003a, 2003b) explained that affect dysregulation is central to almost all forms of psychopathology, so therapeutic interventions that address this crucial deficit will have wide application across the psychodiagnostic spectrum.

The relational component consists of systematic exploration of heartfelt feelings in connection with key attachment figures and other important persons in their social world. Our most heartfelt emotions do not develop in a vacuum. They develop in an interpersonal context. Our strongest emotions tend to be elicited in relation to our key attachment figures. Witness the outpouring of the most intense human emotions when an attachment bond is broken.

In the HFS, the relational component is accomplished in two ways. Typically, I ask the children to color the heart in relation to a very specific relational issue, such as, "Color in the heart according to how you felt when Daddy got mad and left the house last night." The second way the relational component is emphasized in the HFS is in the follow-up questions. Some of the questions are related to the expressive (E) component such as, "Which feeling was the strongest?" or "What feeling is the hardest for you to express?" Another group of follow-up questions, however, are specifically focused on relational (R) issues such as, "Who in the family would agree with your choice of the emotion that is expressed the least in the family?" or "What emotion is most uncomfortable for you to express and who else in the family is uncomfortable expressing that same emotion?" The social context is critical. Some children get angry at school but not at home, others get angry at home but rarely at school. In the HFCCS, the cards are divided into two succinct sets, the *Expressive* and *Relational,* to also emphasize these two key components.

The heart has long symbolized the spiritual, emotional, or moral core of a human being. The word heart has been used poetically in many cultures to represent the soul and stylized depictions of the heart are frequent symbols of love. This stylized shape of the heart is typically colored red, suggesting both blood and, in many cultures, passion and strong emotion. In J. C. Cooper's (1978) book, *An Illustrated Encyclopedia of Traditional Symbols,* the heart is described as, "The centre of being, both physical and spiritual; the divine presence at the centre. The heart represents the 'central' wisdom of feeling as opposed to the head-wisdom of reason; both are intelligence, but the heart is also compassion; understanding; love; charity; it contains the life-blood" (p. 82). A biblical passage expresses this poetically, "Keep and guard your heart with all vigilance and above all that you guard, for out of it flows the springs of life" (Proverbs 4:23).

Neurobiological research as reported by Siegel (1999) has revealed that the heart is not just a romantic or poetic symbol of our deeply held feelings; it has been discovered that there are neural networks surrounding the heart that are responsive to the status of our relationships and attachments to others.

Directions for the "Heartfelt Feelings Strategy"

The therapist instructs the child to pick a color for each of the emotions listed at the bottom of the heart. The child is encouraged to add any other feelings in the blanks and more blanks can be added for those creative children who wish to add still more emotions. The children are then asked to color in the heart their heartfelt feelings in relation to a specific event, such as "when Dad hit mom" or "my brother moved out" or "my teacher yelled at me in front of my class." The children are told to color in the heart according to how much they felt each of the chosen feelings. Because proportion is a difficult concept for children it is useful for the therapist to demonstrate. The therapist can say, "Let me give you an example of heartfelt feelings. I can remember when I was a child that once I did not get invited to a birthday party by a classmate whom I considered to be a friend. I felt hurt, sad, mad, and disappointed. I pick purple to show my hurt. Because that was the feeling I had the most, I am going to color in the heart with more purple than any other color. But I was also mad. I pick red for mad so I will color in the heart with red but not as much as purple because I felt hurt more than mad. I also felt sad, but not as much as hurt and mad. I pick blue for sad so I am going to color in the heart with blue but not as much as red because I was more mad than sad. Finally, I was a little disappointed in my friend. I pick brown for disappointment so I am going to put in just a little brown because I did not feel that as strongly as I felt hurt, mad, and sad. Now I would like you to pick a color for each feeling and then to color in your heart according to how much you felt each of your feelings when . . ." The drawing is then used as a springboard to pursue these feelings in depth.

Walter Bonime emphasized in psychoanalytic supervision of my work the importance for the analyst or therapist to pursue the many shades, variations, and nuances of feelings. He explained that feelings are like "chords in music, not single notes" and the richness of a person's personality is elucidated

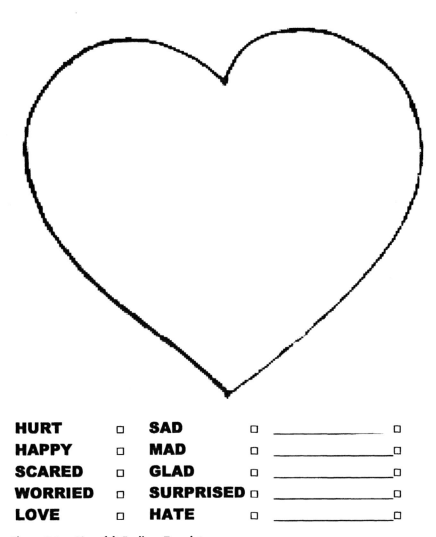

HEARTFELT FEELINGS STRATEGY

HURT	☐	SAD	☐	_____	☐
HAPPY	☐	MAD	☐	_____	☐
SCARED	☐	GLAD	☐	_____	☐
WORRIED	☐	SURPRISED	☐	_____	☐
LOVE	☐	HATE	☐	_____	☐

Figure 2.1.   Heartfelt Feelings Template

by the exploration of the idiosyncratic composition of their affective life and their unique emotional responses to a given situation. Typically, when children are asked what they were feeling in a specific situation they will reply with one predominant feeling, "Oh, I was mad," or "It made me sad." It is a serious error for the child therapist to stop there, because a great deal of information is missed, if the initial meager responses of the child are accepted as complete. The therapist can explain, "Usually kids have more than just one feeling when something upsetting occurs, what else did you feel when this happened?"

Follow-Up Sample Questions

Please note: The questions are either in the expressive (E) or relational (R) domains and are marked as such at the end of each question. The follow-up questions are designed to engage both the cognitive and emotional realm of the child through inquiry and dialogue that evokes logic, reasoning, reflection, perspective-taking, and meaning-making and also the emotional sphere by focusing on heartfelt matters and attachments.

1. What feeling is the strongest, most deeply felt in your coloring of the heart? (E)
2. What led you to pick that feeling over the other feelings? (E)
3. What feeling comes second in your coloring the heart? (E)
4. What led you to pick that feeling next? (E)
5. What feeling comes next? (E)
6. What is the reason for picking that one? (E)
7. What feeling is shown the least in your coloring of the heart? (E)
8. What feeling or feelings are left out altogether in your coloring of the heart? (E)
9. What can be learned about your coloring of the heart about your heartfelt feelings? (E)
10. Did you tell anyone about your heartfelt feelings? (R)
11. If you didn't tell who would be the best person to tell? (R)
12. What feelings are the easiest for you to share with others? (R)
13. What feelings are the hardest for you to share with others? (R)
14. What feeling in your coloring of the heart makes you the most uncomfortable and who else in the family is uncomfortable expressing that emotion? (R)
15. If you had to pick just one feeling, which one do you think is expressed most often in your family? (R)

16. If you had to pick just one feeling that best fits you, what one would it be? (E)
17. If you had to pick just one feeling that best fits each member of your family, what one would you pick for each person? (R)
18. If you had to pick just one feeling that best fits your relationship with each member of the family, what feeling would you pick for each relationship? (R)
19. If you had to pick just one feeling that is expressed the least in the family which one would you pick? (R)
20. Who in the family would agree with your choice of the emotion that is expressed the least in the family? (R)
21. What made you pick that feeling and who in the family would disagree with your pick? (R)
22. Who in the family expresses anger the most? (R)
23. Who in the family has the hardest time expressing anger? (R)
24. Who in the family expresses affection the most? (R)
25. Who in the family shows the most sadness? (R)
26. Who in the family shows the most happiness? (R)
27. Who in the family would be the first to notice if you were sad? (R)
28. Who in the family would be most upset or worried if you were sad? (R)
29. Who in the family would be the first to notice if you were angry? (R)
30. Who in the family would be most upset if you were angry? (R)
31. Who would you go to first in the family if you were worried? (R)
32. Who would you go to first in the family if you were scared? (R)
33. Who in the family would you go to first if you were sad? (R)
34. Who in the family would you want to tell first if you were happy? (R)
35. Who in the family would you want to tell first if you were hurt? (R)

Clinical Illustration

The nine-year-old boy who was embroiled in parental warfare chose red to depict his mad feelings and the greater portion of the heart is covered in red. The next largest proportion of the heart is colored blue, the color he chose for sad. Another significant proportion is colored approximately in equal amounts with orange and purple. He chose orange to represent his scared feelings and purple to symbolize his sad feelings. Finally a smaller portion of the heart was colored brown, the color he chose to represent worry. His

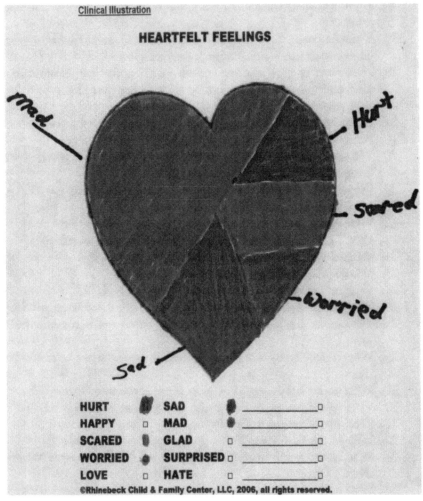

Figure 2.2.   Clinical Illustrations of the HFS

coloring of the heart became a springboard to discuss each of these feelings using some of the sample questions provided above.

Additional Clinical Applications

Generic Application   A modification of this technique is to use it in the same manner as O'Connor's (1983) "Color-Your-Life" strategy and tell the children to pretend that the heart represents their whole life so far. They then are told to color in the heartfelt feelings according to how much of each they have experienced in their life to this point. As mentioned previously, the abstract nature of this application will make it difficult for children younger than nine to comply but some exceptional children will be able to do it.

Relational Applications   An alternative is to ask children to use the heartfelt feelings technique to color in their feelings according to how deeply they have felt their chosen feelings in relation to their family. Another option would be to ask them to color in the heart according to their feelings toward each family member. In that case the youngsters would color a separate heart for each member of the family according to their feelings. In these latter two options the HFS is being used in a relational framework consistent with family systems theory.

Taking the Child's "Emotional Pulse"   Still another application of this strategy that has been found clinically useful is to use it to take the child's "emotional pulse." In this adaptation, the therapist lets the child know early on in therapy process that the child will be asked at various points in the therapy to color in the heart according to how they are feeling at that point in time. If for example, a child is caught in the middle of a bitter divorce and custody battle, the use of the HFS will often capture and depict the most deeply held feelings for the child at any one point along the way. During the throes of the parent battle within the courts, the child will often emphasize fear, anger, and worry in their coloring of the heart. When the conflict is less pronounced the child might depict these emotions as less intense and even include some positive emotions as a result of the temporary relief.

For children who are weary and battle scarred from the constant vindictive actions between the parents, HFS allows them an artistic and symbolic means of expression that for many children is more comfortable and less threatening than direct verbal expression. It also allows in most cases for verbal follow-up of the emotions depicted in the heart. Because the communication with the therapist takes place within the structure afforded by this strategy, the kids are often empowered to elaborate more on their feelings than they would typically do in response to direct questioning.

Working through Termination Feelings   Another clinical application is preparing children for termination of therapy. The children are instructed to color in the heart according to how they feel about ending therapy. This then becomes a jumping off place to explore these feelings in more depth. Likewise, therapists can choose to color in a heart expressing their feelings about working with the child and give it to the child at the last session. Additional tools in working through termination were previously delineated (Crenshaw, 2006b; Crenshaw and Mordock, 2005a).

Exploring Countertransference   Another application is to use the HFS to explore countertransference feelings. In my own clinical work as well as in supervision of other child therapists I have colored or asked the therapist-supervisee to color the heart according to the strength of their various heartfelt feelings in relation to the therapeutic work with a specific child or family.

The tool can be used as an ongoing self-monitoring process at the beginning, in middle stages, and then again toward the end of therapy, or it can be employed when the therapist feels "stuck" or when either therapist or supervisor notes a disproportionate emotional response to the client.

Often the therapist-supervisee is astonished when they apportion their feelings according to their intensity. Sometimes they are surprised by an emotion they depict in the heart of which they were previously unaware. This can lead to useful reflection, a meaningful exchange with supervisor, and in some cases an issue to pursue in their personal therapy. If for example, anger predominates in their depiction of their heartfelt feelings, it is important to explore what evokes such anger in working with this child. They may discover that the trigger is the child's refusal to expose any vulnerability or dependency; it may lead the therapist in personal therapy to explore the need to be needed by the child. Many young and inexperienced therapists fall prey to the need to prove their adequacy and skills as a beginning therapist and become enraged when the child does not cooperate or make progress. This can become a self-reinforcing disruptive process since the pressure the therapist feels to prove competence is experienced by the child and interferes with the natural pace of healing for the client.

This application is new but shows potential as a powerful tool in self-examination of the therapist's countertransference feelings or as a tool in the supervision process (for additional play therapy strategies for working with countertransference see Gil & Rubin, 2005).

Modifications Created by Children   Children sometimes add their own creative modifications to this technique. When asked to color in their heartfelt feelings in relation to their parents, children will sometimes draw a line down the middle of the heart. They depict and color their separate feelings toward each parent. This is an interesting, spontaneous modification because it clearly demonstrates the loyalty of the child to both parents and the special place they both occupy in the child's heart.

Another creative adaptation demonstrated by some children whose parents are in high-conflict marriages or divorces is to split the two halves of the heart apart, vividly expressing the split loyalties that these youngsters struggle with on an ongoing basis. Anna Freud pointed out more than sixty years ago that if the parents hate each other the child can only love one parent. Under these conditions they feel coerced to choose between their parents. The loyalties may shift rapidly and frequently but kids truly believe that under these circumstances it is impossible to love both parents at the same time.

The Therapeutic Use of Symbols

A modification of the "Heartfelt Feelings Strategy," particularly when children are unable to verbally elaborate on the feelings depicted in the coloring of the heart shape, is to ask them to pick a symbol from a group of miniatures to go with each of the feelings depicted and to place the symbol on top of the colored regions of the heart. In some cases, the visual impact of the symbols will enable children to expand on their feelings when the therapist explores with them the question of why they picked a given symbol for each of the represented feelings and if not, the symbol itself may "speak" volumes.

THE "HEARTFELT FEELINGS COLORING CARD STRATEGIES" (HFCCS) (CHILDREN AGES 4 TO 17)

Purpose: *The Heartfelt Feelings Coloring Card Strategies (HFCCS) are additional tools for child therapists designed to provide a psychoeducational component that offers opportunities for children in therapy to identify, label, and express their heartfelt feelings (Expressive Series) and another component (Relational Series) that facilitates the process of children expressing and exploring their heartfelt feelings in relation to the key attachments and important others in their interpersonal world.*

I collaborated with Paul Marciano, PhD, CEO and founder of the Coloring Card Company, in this expansion of the original "Heartfelt Feelings Strategy." The company specializes in greeting cards created by child artists and colored by children before giving them to others and the HFCCS are presented in the format akin to greeting cards. On the front of the card is the heart shape; on the inside of the card are directives to children to write about the context of their feelings (Expressive) or to write a note to the person chosen according to directives (Relational). The back of the card contains a place for the child's name and the date.

The Expressive Series

The HFCCS Kit (Crenshaw, 2007a) consists of a Clinical Manual and 20 Expressive Cards and 20 Relational Cards. Therapists can use the cards in a sequential manner because the emotions recommended for the Expressive Cards early in the series are intended for younger children (ages four to six), while feelings later in the sequence are intended for older children (ages nine and older). Unlike the "Heartfelt Feelings Strategy" or "Color-Your-Heart," "Feelings Map," and "Color-Your-Life" techniques, this series does not require children to deal with proportion. While children often experience mixed, ambivalent, and conflicting feelings, they find it hard to articulate such feelings and even harder to quantify the proportions of each. In the "Heartfelt Feelings Strategy," as previously mentioned, it is not typically recommended for children under the age of nine for that reason. The HFCCS is uniquely designed to give children from preschool age upward opportunities in identifying, labeling, and expressing a wide range of increasingly complex and sophisticated emotions. The HFCCS expressive series offers children a choice of drawing their own heart or using the one provided on the front of the card. This is a feature not included in other therapeutic strategies using the heart shape.

Directions for the Expressive Series

On the left panel of the inside of the card, the child is presented with the statement, "My heart is filled with <u>happiness</u>" (or one of the other feelings chosen by the child or therapist). Then the child picks a color for happiness from the box of crayons. At that point the child decides whether to color the heart on the front of the card or draw his or her own in the space provided on the left inside panel of the card, and to color it using the color chosen. The next step takes place on the right panel on the inside of the card. The child is presented with the statement, "My heart is filled with happiness when:

_____

_____

_____

_____

Some children, particularly older ones, will want to do the writing themselves, while more of the younger ones will want or need the therapist to do the writing in the space and lines provided on the card. This step requires the child to provide some context for the particular feeling, in this example, happiness. More importantly, it provides a springboard for therapeutic dialogue about the heartfelt feelings of the child. This is where child therapists show their true mettle. It is in the sensitive exploration of the feelings and their many variations using this exercise as a starting point that enables children little by little to gain enough trust with the therapist to share more of their emotional and relational world. As the child and therapist proceed through the series the emotions may in some cases be more threatening, negative, and difficult to talk about but by then it is expected that the child will have gained sufficient trust in the therapist that he or she will feel safe and more open to discussing such feelings. Some of the more complex and sophisticated emotions that come later in the sequence would be reserved primarily for older children. While younger children are not expected to know the more sophisticated emotions, some will be motivated to learn them and in those cases the HFCCS can be a useful teaching tool to expand the child's feelings vocabulary.

It is difficult to set an arbitrary upper age limit on the HFCCS and it may vary for the expressive and the relational components. The HFCCS and the HFS can be used with teens looking for a face-saving way to participate in therapy when they find the whole process threatening. One eighteen-year-old expressed the sentiment, "I wished they'd had something like this when I went to therapy as a kid, this is great." Each child therapist will have to determine with a given child what the upper age limit for the usefulness of these tools is for that specific youngster.

Therapists can, of course, substitute other emotions that they think would be specifically relevant for a given child and arrange them in a sequence from simple to complex. In the columns below some of the feelings are listed that the therapist can use in the Expressive Series with the words in the first column expected to be more useful for younger children and as the list proceeds to more complex emotions, those will be better suited to older children.

Expressive Series: "My heart is filled with _____."

Column 1	Column 2	Column 3	Column 4
Happiness	Boredom	Jealousy	Contentment
Gladness	Worry	Pain	Disgust
Anger	Delight	Joy	Embarrassment
Sadness	Humiliation	Relief	Disappointment
Fear	Gratitude	Despair	Admiration
Surprise	Grief	Wonder	Appreciation
Love	Annoyance	Pride	Curiosity
Hurt	Terror	Shame	Satisfaction
Hope	Irritation	Envy	Excitement
Guilt	Excitement	Confusion	Distress

Clinical Example

A nine-year-old boy colored the heart blue, a color he picked for sadness then explained why his heart was filled with sadness. He was missing his father who had moved away and he feared that his father had forgotten about him. He wrote on the inside of the card, "I think you forget about me. When my mom went to court I thought you might remember me and maybe you did." I find this card especially sad. When his mother went to court to try and collect overdue child support, the child wonders if that occasion would remind his dad that he had a son.

Figure 2.3. HFCCS Template for Front of the Card

My heart is filled with _____
and I pick the color _____ for this
feeling.

Please color the heart on the front of the
card or draw your own heart below with the
color you picked.

My heart was once filled with this feeling
when . . .

_____
_____
_____
_____
_____
_____
_____
_____
_____
_____
_____
_____
_____

Figure 2.4.   HFCCS Template for Inside Panels of the Expressive Card

Another boy, eight years old, colored the heart on the front of the HFCCS card blue for sadness but he went a step further and drew tears flowing down from the heart. On the inside he wrote a note to his parents, "When you fight, I am sad because I love you guys. Sometimes I get scared that you two are going to burst with anger and the police will come and take me and Sherry [fictitious name for his sister] to a foster home." While such important and heartfelt feelings may well have emerged in therapy eventually, the HFCCS, literally and figuratively, goes directly to the heart of the child's feelings in a therapeutic activity that facilitates communication of such feelings between child and therapist.

Background of the Relational Series

The relational series builds on the work of Liana Lowenstein (2006) who uses a strategy involving the heart shape called "Always in My Heart" (Lowenstein, 2006, p. 109). Lowenstein asks children to cut out the shape of a heart that she makes available on the above page of her book. She then asks them to draw a picture of their special person inside the heart and, if they wish, to decorate the heart. She states to the children, "Let it remind you that your special person who died is always in your heart" (p. 109). This is a poignant way to symbolize the timeless attachment that goes on forever with those whom we love.

Using the heart on the front of this card or a heart that you draw below, please draw

_____

_____

You may then color your heart if you wish.

Please write a note to the person you picked. If you prefer, you can tell the story of why you picked this person.

_____

_____

_____

_____

_____

_____

_____

_____

_____

_____

_____

Figure 2.5.   HFCCS Template for Inside Panels of the Expressive Card

Relational Series: Key Attachments

Purpose: *The goal of the Key Attachments strategy is to explore the child's heart-felt feelings in relation to the important people in the child's family, school, social, and community life. An additional goal is to expand the therapeutic dialogue about the child's positive relationships as well as any conflicts, barriers, or cut-offs impacting emotionally on the child and family.*

In the Key Attachments strategy, the children draw (inside the heart provided on the front of the card or within the heart they choose to draw) a person, for example, <u>whom they can most easily go to when they are in trouble.</u> I support the strategy proposed by Lowenstein (2006) to draw the image of the person even if it is a stick figure rather than simply write the name of the person because images are more evocative of feelings than words (Crenshaw, 2006b).

If a child is inhibited about drawing, I urge readers to follow the guidelines that Cathy Malchiodi (1998) provided for overcoming so-called resistance in children to drawing. The therapist can demonstrate for the child the drawing of a person even if the therapist does a stick figure. Sometimes it can be done collaboratively, "I'll start and you can help me finish it." If the child still refuses after employing the strategies that Malchiodi suggested, the child can name the person rather than forgo the strategy altogether but it is important not to yield too quickly because most children will respond to encouragement to draw. Another alternative to simply naming the person is to ask the child to select a miniature to place in the heart to symbolize the person.

The Relational Series may be more threatening to the child because it is a tool to explore heartfelt feelings toward key attachment figures and may trigger loyalty conflicts. If the child's reluctance is not just toward the drawing requirement but toward the whole process, it is recommended that the resistance be respected. The child can be told, "We will do this at another time, when it will be more comfortable for you."

Children feel safer in therapy when their defenses are honored and paradoxically the therapy moves quicker under those conditions. The statement above not only respects the pace at which they need to go, but it plants the firm expectation, "We will come back to this at a time that is more comfortable for you." Any child, any adult for that matter, would prefer to avoid the "hard stuff" altogether. Honoring the defenses doesn't mean, "We'll just forget about this." Rather it indicates, "We will come back to it when you are ready." One of the key factors in evaluating readiness is the strength of the therapeutic alliance, which provides the safe context for therapeutic exploration. If the child is reluctant to engage in either the expressive or relational components, it may signify that the child doesn't yet trust enough in the therapeutic relationship to risk such exploration and that building the therapeutic alliance should be the priority focus.

The next step in the therapeutic application of the relational series is to ask the child to write a note to the person on the right panel of the inside of the card. The child in some cases will want to do the writing, while other children will prefer to tell the story of why they chose this particular person. In that instance the therapist will write the story in the space provided or the child may choose to dictate a note to the person that the therapist writes. The efficacy of this strategy will depend on the skill and experience of the child therapist in expanding on what the child gives, which in the beginning may be rather meager but can serve as a starting point for therapeutic exploration of their primary attachments.

The relational series directives deliberately avoid using instructions that would pursue overt destructiveness in relationships with key attachment figures because I was concerned that it would be too threatening to children. Also, it would require disclosure perhaps before the child is ready to acknowledge such events or face the full range of consequences that would stem from such disclosure. In addition, it avoids the risk of misinterpretation by the child of the task requirements or the therapist's misinterpreting the child's responses to the task that in some instances may offer skimpy or ambiguous information about the child's relationships. Any interpretation of destructiveness in the child's family or interpersonal relationships should be based on thorough exploration of those relationships that this series may serve as a springboard to facilitate.

While directives for the relational cards do not directly ask children about anyone in their life who hurts them physically or emotionally, the cards will encourage such a thorough examination of the child's interpersonal world that any such direct harm would likely be shared by the child in the ensuing discussions between child and therapist. Further, because most of the relational cards pull for positive themes and attachments that most children will find comfortable discussing with the therapist, such sharing will strengthen the bond between the child and therapist and if the child is at risk of harm in any of his relationships, it is more likely to be disclosed in the context of the enhanced, secure therapeutic alliance.

Directives for the Relational Cards: Key Attachments

"Draw within the heart on the front or in the heart you have drawn . . ."

1. "Someone who will be in your heart forever."
2. "Other persons you want to include in your heart."

3. "A person who is now outside your heart that was once inside."
4. "A person who is outside your heart that you wish to be inside."
5. "The person you can most easily talk to."
6. "The person that you would go to if you were in trouble."
7. "A person who makes you safe."
8. "A person you deeply respect."
9. "A person that you love."
10. "A person whom you trust."
11. "The person whom you would want with you when you are sick."
12. "The person you worry about the most."
13. "A person who is kind-hearted."
14. "A person who is very forgiving."
15. "A person with a loving heart."
16. "A person with a generous heart."
17. "A person with a patient heart."
18. "A person with a broken heart."
19. "A person with an understanding heart."
20. "A person with a lonely heart."
21. "The person who is most encouraging to you."
22. "The person who is most supportive of you."
23. "A person you admire."
24. "A person to whom you owe gratitude."
25. "The teacher who is most helpful to you."
26. "The person who is most helpful to you."
27. "The pet that is most special to you."
28. "The friend that is most special to you."
29. "The adult who is the most helpful to you."
30. "The teacher who is most special to you."
31. "The person you miss the most."
32. "A person you have shown great kindness toward."
33. "A person you have shown great caring toward."
34. "A person who has shown unusual courage."
35. "A person who has shown great determination.
36. "A person who will accept you no matter what."
37. "The person you know with the best sense of humor."
38. "The person who understands you best."
39. "The person who is most loyal to you."
40. "The person that you try the hardest to please."

Please note: For many of the directives above, for example, "A person that you love," the child may wish to do more than one card. This would reinforce and highlight the strength of the child's attachments.

Clinical Example

An eight-year-old boy drew his mother in the heart on the front of the card and then wrote on the inside of the HFCCS card, "Mommy, I love you." Because he suffered a series of devastating losses, the importance of his mother as a consistent attachment figure in his life took on renewed significance. In the ensuing therapeutic exchange he talked about these recent losses in more depth and with more genuine feeling than was possible for him to do prior. This strategy brings into clear focus for both the child and therapist the key attachments in the child's life and the related heartfelt feelings that youth often can't easily share.

Additional Relational Strategies

Relational Series: "Circle of Caring"   **Purpose:** *The goal of the "Circle of Caring" relational series is to solidify in the mind of children the circle of people who love and care for them and who are available as sources of support and help when needed. When children are in the throes of emotional crises they can easily lose sight of the external support system available to them. Another goal would be to expand the "Circle of Caring" by identifying other trustworthy adults who care and support the child.*

Background   A family can be defined as a circle of people who care about you. Children who lack biological relatives who care about them can still have a family if viewed as a circle of people who care about them, helps, and supports them. This expanded view of family is especially important to children who are adopted or who are placed in foster care and at least temporarily separated from their biological families. Even children living in intact families benefit from identifying, highlighting, and expanding their circle of caring. The more caring connections we have with others, the richer our lives.

Directives to the Child   "Please draw in the heart on the front of the card or in the heart you draw below (in the space provided on the left inside panel of the Relational Series Card) a picture of one of the people who cares about you. This person has shown you that she or he really cares about you and deserves to be in your 'circle of caring'."

After drawing the person the child is asked to "Please write a note to this person or tell the story of why you picked this person to be in your 'circle of caring'." In the latter case, the therapist would write the story on the lines provided on the right hand panel of the inside of the Relational Card. When the child has drawn as many people as he or she can think of to put into the "circle of caring" the therapist can further expand the dialogue by moving into symbol work.

"Circle of Caring" Symbol Work   The therapist can ask the child to please pick a symbol from a group of miniatures to represent self. Then the therapist

would ask the child to arrange the "Circle of Caring" cards in a circle around the symbol chosen for self. This offers a dramatic visual representation of the child's "circle of caring." The dialogue can be further expanded by asking the child to pick a symbol for each of the people in his or her "circle of caring." It should be mentioned that many children will want to include pets in their "circle of caring," which is okay and in this case they would pick a symbol to represent the pet. The visual impact of the symbols representing their "circle of caring" further solidifies in their minds and hearts the interpersonal resources available to them.

The therapeutic dialogue can be enriched further by inquiring as to why the child picked the particular symbol to represent each of the people and/or pets in his or her circle. Because of the power of symbol and image to evoke feeling, it can be rather moving when children visually survey the surrounding circle of caring people and/or pets. It is also more likely that these resources will stick in their minds during crisis times because of the visual/symbolic depiction of their resources as well as the drawing and note writing activities related to their circle.

Exploring Countertransference   Using the Relational Cards, the supervisees are asked to draw an image in the heart on the front of the card that comes to mind when they think of a troubling therapy case. It may be a child who is always testing limits or provokes anxiety and anguish in the therapist. The image could be anything that comes to mind for the therapist but in some cases it is a picture of the child or the child and the therapist in some kind of struggle with each other. In one case the image drawn by the therapist was of her pushing a heavy rock up a hill expressing her exhaustion and utter frustration in her efforts to help a seven-year-old boy who made a practice of thwarting her efforts. In the latter instance it became clear that the image of pushing the heavy rock up the hill was related to far more than her frustration with this particular child. It was related to depression she had been battling and this image was the jumpstart she needed to seek her own therapy to address her mood disorder. Therapy with acting-out and provocative youngsters is often fraught with anxiety and can place an emotional strain on the therapist.

The next step with the HFCCS Relational Cards is to write a note on the inside of the card to the child or the family. Sometimes I alter the instructions and ask them to write a note to the supervisor summarizing their feelings as symbolized in the image they drew within the heart. Therapists can use the HFS and HFCCS not only in supervision but also as a self-monitoring tool in working with their own reactions in therapy with a wide variety of clinical cases.

Additional variations of the HFCCS Relational strategies are described in later chapters. "Unsung Heroes and Heroines" is described in Chapter 4; "Empathy for Self and Others" is detailed in Chapter 6; and "Hellos and Goodbyes" is presented in Chapter 8.

How These Strategies Enhance the Therapy Process

The HFS and HFCCS strategies can further the process of therapy in multiple ways. When children externalize their feelings in an artistic manner, in this instance by coloring in a heart, it is easier to talk about them. It also enables the therapist to promote a collaborative approach to exploring and understanding the child's feelings. When the child and therapist are both looking at the colored-in heart shape, they are together studying each of the feelings portrayed along with the proportions of each. In addition, when feelings are artistically depicted on paper, the child and therapist can stand back and together view them in an objective manner. This can lead the child to view these emotions in a different perspective. Often they are surprised when they look at the heart shape and see some of the feelings portrayed or they may become aware of just how strongly they feel certain feelings. Finally, feelings externalized in the form of the colored heart shape and examined with the therapist are often experienced by the child as more manageable, than feelings unexpressed and not well understood.

I can't emphasize enough that these tools are not healing interventions in themselves; rather, they can lead to enriching the therapeutic dialogue; enhance empathy—an empirically supported therapeutic relationship factor (Norcross, 2001)—and sharing between child and therapist, which does contribute to healing; and further strengthen the therapeutic alliance, yet another potent contributor to healing.

The art of child therapy is to find ways to structure the therapeutic context to make it comfortable for children to communicate their emotional life and relational world to the therapist. What we call resistance, may rather be a therapist's inability to find ways to structure the therapeutic process in a way that enables children to communicate their heartfelt feelings, even when they wish to do so. The HFS and the HFCCS give specific directives to the child that structure the communication around a specific situation or relationship. In addition, in the HFS, specific follow-up questions explore both expressive and relational domains to once again structure the therapeutic exchange and this enables children, even those who are inhibited or guarded, to share more of their heartfelt feelings in relation to situations and people that matter most.

Resources for Clinicians for Materials Described in This Chapter

The Heartfelt Coloring Cards Strategy (HFCCS) Kit can be obtained from the Coloring Card Company (www.coloringcardcompany.com) or (908) 237-2500; email@coloringcardcompany.com. The Kit contains a Clinical Manual that covers instructions and background of both the HFS and the HFCCS and a set of Expressive Cards (20) and a set of Relational Cards (20). Ten percent of sales are donated to the Children's Foundation of the Astor Home for Children, which has as its motto: ". . . because every child deserves a childhood."

The Therapeutic Use of Symbols to Engage Children and Adolescents

𝒫urpose: This group of strategies, along with other symbol strategies in this book, are an extension of the therapeutic use of symbols described previously (Crenshaw, 2006b). Symbols tend to be more powerful than words. Images preceded words in preverbal life. This group of strategies is based on associative activity to symbols and to evocative word stimuli. The symbol strategies offer a window into the inner life of a child and adolescent, thereby increasing understanding and empathy. Children don't always understand what is hurting inside, thus what may appear as "resistance" is really their lack of awareness of what is wrong. The symbol tools may assist the therapist in learning about the inner pain when the child is unable to tell us.

THE "SYMBOL ASSOCIATION THERAPY STRATEGIES" (SATS)

The use of symbols and the associative responses they evoke both cognitively and emotionally serve as a springboard for further exploration in a determined effort to understand and connect in a meaningful way with the child or adolescent in therapy. Like the HFS and the HFCCS, the SATS has both *Expressive* and *Relational* domains.

These strategies are not intended to be part of a formal assessment process. As a result, however, of sampling the child's thought process in repeated associative activity, if concerns arise then the child should be referred for an intellectual, cognitive, and/or personality assessment. While this strategy like the others was developed with a Relational Therapy framework in mind, it does not depend on a particular therapeutic orientation. Jungian therapists will approach the understanding of the symbols consistent with their understanding of the universal meaning of certain symbols. My approach to symbols stems from my analytic supervision with Walter Bonime who in his classic book, *The Clinical Use of Dreams* (1962), took the approach that symbols can't be assumed to have universal meaning, rather the meaning for a specific symbol for a particular person may well be idiosyncratic and rooted in their unique life experiences. The meaning would thus need to be pursued with the client in each instance.

Background of the SATS

The evocative power of symbol enjoys a long and rich tradition in psychotherapy especially in sand play therapy and in Jungian analysis. Eliana Gil (2006) combined the evocative power of symbol with one of family therapy's time-honored tools, the family genogram, to create the individual and family play genogram. Instead of names being placed in the diagram of the family's history, the child or family selects a symbol from a group of miniatures to represent each family member. Gil and Rubin (2005) employ symbols as powerful tools in working with countertransference issues in child and family therapy. Many other creative approaches to the use of symbols in therapy are described by Lois Carey (1998; 2006) and DeDomenico (1999) in sand play therapy, building on the pioneering work in sand play therapy by Margaret Lowenfeld (1939; 1979) and Dora Kalff (1971; 1980).

Theodore Kahn, an Air Force psychologist, created the Kahn Test of Symbol Arrangement (KTSA) (Kahn, 1957; Kahn and Murphy, 1958). The test is rarely used today but was once used as a tool for personality assessment. Kahn (1951) explained that the original idea of using plastic shapes of common objects for personality diagnosis occurred when he observed people purchasing such objects in a Los Angeles hobby store. Originally Kahn assembled a huge collection of such plastic trinkets and then reduced the group down to 15 based on multiple selection criteria. Kahn (1951) explained, "Versatility and variety of cultural associations were among the criteria used in the retention of specific items. Thus the horse shapes were eliminated, the dog shapes retained, since the latter offered a wider scope of acceptance and rejectance. The faithfulness and loyalty of the dog is at one end—house pet, sled-puller, watchdog, and cattle-corraller is near the center—and being called the son of a female canine, undoubtedly, is at the other end of the acceptance-rejection continuum. Similarly, associations for the butterfly ranged from beauty to fickleness, and for the anchor, from travel and thus freedom of action to something that ties one down and thus destroys freedom of action" (p. 439).

Kahn also considered popularity of color and shape of the objects as measured by frequency of occurrence in magazine advertisements and in the flags of the countries of the United Nations. While some objects in the retained items are similar, most are also different by virtue of size, shape, or color. In the end Kahn ended up with the following fifteen objects: Anchor—blue plastic; Butterfly—brown plastic; Butterfly—transparent plastic; Circle—transparent plastic; Cross—black plastic; Dog—black plastic; Dog (smaller)—black plastic; Dog (smaller)—white plastic; Heart—blue plastic; Heart (larger) transparent plastic; Heart (smaller)—red plastic; Parrot—green plastic; Star—transparent plastic; Star—two identical smaller red translucent plastic. The KTSA also consists of a brown felt strip divided into fifteen equal segments. Kahn intended the felt strip to represent the environment over which the test subject had no control. The squares numbering from one to fifteen on the strip as Kahn explained, "Conform to the consecutiveness imposed on life by the immutable progression of time" (Kahn, 1951, p. 440).

In spite of three favorable critical reviews (L'Abate and Craddick, 1965; Craddick and L'Abate, 1972; and Ammons and Ammons, 1980), the KTSA, consistent with the decline of the popularity of projective techniques in general in recent years, has virtually disappeared from contemporary use as a projective technique. In a literature search, I could find only two articles published on the KTSA in the 1990s, the last of which was in 1998.

A final task in the KTSA testing procedure entailed instructing clients to sort the fifteen symbols into six different categories that consisted of three positive categories: LOVE, GOOD, and LIVING and three negative categories: HATE, BAD, and DEAD. In the sorting task the clients could put as many symbols of the fifteen on any category they wished or they could leave any category blank as long as they used the fifteen symbols distributed in whatever way they chose. This is what gave me the idea of creating my own symbol-sorting strategy not for the purpose of diagnosis or assessment but as a way of engaging the child or adolescent in meaningful therapeutic conversation. By using symbols that are culturally popular and in some cases, emotionally evocative, these tools can jumpstart the therapy process or help restart it when it has bogged down.

One clear difference between Kahn's procedure on the symbol sorting task is that in the SATS Strategy #1 and Strategy #2, the client is asked to pick the one symbol that best fits a given category and then to state the reasons for making that selection. The SATS Strategy #3 follows the lead of the KTSA sorting task in inviting the client to put as many or few or none of the symbols as he or she wishes on the Relational Domains word stimuli.

Materials Needed

All of the Symbol Association Sheets and Recording Sheets are contained in the SATS Clinical Manual (Crenshaw, in press a). Many child, adolescent, and family therapists will already have a collection of miniatures that they use in sand play therapy or in symbol work in child therapy. If the therapist does not have such a collection, the Self Esteem Shop (see resources for clinicians at the end of this chapter) has made available a collection of small plastic miniatures called the SATS Basic Symbol Set. The collection contains fifty miniatures that provide children with adequate choices but do not overwhelm them with too many choices. The collection consists of the following symbols: pets consisting of dogs and cats in different sizes and colors; people including a child, baby, school-age boy and girl, and mother and father. The set includes a multicultural family as well as Caucasian one, making for a total of twelve people; farm animals of different kinds and sizes, as well as jungle animals. The remaining collection consists of hearts of different colors and sizes, stars, butterflies, flowers, a tree, a house, a gun, a knife, and religious symbols. Consistent with Kahn's selection of symbols in the KTSA, a parrot and an anchor are included as well.

The Symbol Association Sheets for strategies #1 and #2 contain fifteen words on each sheet covering a broad range of emotionally evocative words derived from empirical research on emotionally significant and neutral words in experimental psychology (Algom, Chajut, and Lev, 2004; Anderson, 2005; Drobes, Elibero, and Evans, 2006; Gruhn, Smith, and Baltes, 2005; Hadley and MacKay, 2006). Furthermore, this research has identified words that have positive and negative emotional valence among the emotionally significant words. It has been shown in these studies that emotionally significant words, particularly of negative valence, shape perceptual experience by commanding greater attentional and processing priority.

For the purposes of the SATS, this literature was combed not to study perceptual processes per se, but rather to identify words used in these experimental studies with emotional significance, both positive and negative. Words that would be difficult for school-age children were eliminated and no taboo words were included. The resulting list of seventy-five emotionally evocative words, fifteen on each of five sheets, comprises the Symbol Association Sheets for strategies #1 and #2. The list contains thirty-seven emotionally significant words from the above literature identified to have negative emotional valence and thirty-eight words from the literature identified to have positive emotional valence. No emotionally neutrally words were selected since the objective was to select words that would be emotionally evocative and more likely to elicit meaningful and heartfelt material in the symbol associations that could then be explored in detail in the therapeutic collaboration between child and therapist.

A sample Symbol Association Sheet for strategies #1 and #2 shown in figure 3.1 reveals that the emotionally significant words cover a wide range of emotions and events. A sample Symbol Association Sheet for strategy #3 (Relational Domains) is shown in figure 3.2. By combining the power of symbol with word associations that have been demonstrated in research studies to evoke significant emotion, both positive and negative, this tool should facilitate heartfelt exchange about matters that are truly important to the child and family.

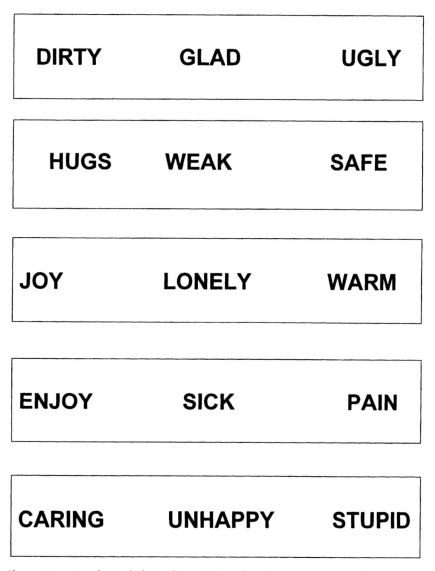

Figure 3.1.   Sample Symbol-Word Association Sheet for Strategies #1 and #2

FAMILY

HOME

Figure 3.2.   Sample Symbol-Word Association Sheet for Strategy #3

Obviously, readers may make their own categories or expand on the ones I offer as they see fit. The possible associative combinations between symbols chosen by the child and evocative stimulus words are endless. Children or families may also suggest new categories thus making this a truly collaborative effort. The strategies can be used not only in individual, but in group and family therapy as well. In either group or family therapy the symbols could be chosen by consensus of the whole group or the group could be divided into sub-groups to decide on the symbol associations.

INSTRUCTIONS FOR THE SATS:
STRATEGY #1 (EXPRESSIVE DOMAIN)

Step 1, the child is asked to pick fifteen symbols of their choice from a collection of miniatures. Step 2, the child is then asked to place the symbols on one of the five Symbol Association Sheets (strategies #1 and #2) contained in the SATS Clinical Manual (Crenshaw, in press a). Fifteen evocative words are presented on each sheet. The child is asked to make the best fit possible for each of the symbols to the evocative words. Step 3 centers on exploring the reasons for the choice of each symbol placed on a given word. The child's responses are recorded on the Symbol Association Recording Sheets contained in the SATS Clinical Manual (Crenshaw, in press a). This is perhaps the most crucial step because this tool is not used or intended for assessment nor for diagnostic purposes but rather for the modest but important goal of furthering therapeutic dialogue with the child in order to understand and appreciate the child's inner life and relational world. Typically one Symbol Association Sheet will take most of a given therapeutic session. The therapist can continue with the next Symbol Association Sheet at a subsequent session if this proves to be a productive therapeutic activity for a given child. Issues of timing and appropriateness of the strategy for a given child are a matter left entirely to the judgment of the therapist.

If the strategy is continued, it is recommended that again the child be invited to choose the fifteen symbols that he/she wants to use from the collection. The child is instructed again to place the symbols on the evocative words that best match. The sense of meaningful and thoughtful work with the symbols is reinforced by the exploration of the reasons behind the child's choices of symbol/word associations. Allowing the child to choose new symbols means the number of possible symbol associations and symbol/word associations are numerous and provides rich material for therapeutic discourse and exploration.

INSTRUCTIONS FOR SATS: STRATEGY #2

In this strategy the child is not required to choose in advance the fifteen symbols but rather to pick one at a time from the entire collection of miniatures the one that best fits with each of the fifteen evocative words on each of the five Symbol Association Sheets. Due to the time element, it is recommended, once again, that only one Symbol Association Sheet be undertaken in any given session. The child's responses are recorded on the Symbol Association Recording Sheets and become the springboard for further therapeutic exchange.

DIRECTIONS FOR SATS:
STRATEGY #3 (RELATIONAL DOMAIN)

The Relational Symbol Associations Sheets in the Workbook are created with just two evocative words printed on each sheet allowing for placement of multiple symbols on each category. The purpose of this relational strategy is to use symbol associations to pursue the child's relational world specifically in relation to three key domains of any child's life: (1) family and home; (2) school; (3) friends and peer relationships. The Relational Symbol Association Sheets are set in front of the child and the child is asked to pick the symbols (one or more) that best match with each of the categories. After placement of the symbols the therapist records on the Symbol Association Recording Sheets (Relational) the names of the symbols and the child's reasons for picking each one. Once again, since the focus is on the key relationships in the child's life, it is expected that exploring the child's choice of symbols and reasoning behind the selections will yield rich clinical material. Another alternative is to ask the child to pick just one symbol for each of the relational associations and record the name of the symbol and the reasons for picking the one symbol on the Symbol Association Recording Sheets for strategy #3.

CLINICAL EXAMPLES

One child, a nine-year-old boy, chose fifteen symbols, all animals, to use in the SATS strategy #1. At the end of the symbol associations and inquiry I asked him if he noticed that he had not chosen any people among the fifteen symbols. He said, "I just like animals." I said, "Perhaps it has nothing at all to do with your choice of all animals but I was wondering if maybe people have let you down or disappointed you." He had suffered two severe relationship traumas that had been a primary focus of the therapy. He said, "Maybe some but I just like animals." He then proceeded to draw two heart-rending drawings depicting the relational traumas. In this case, the portal of entry was not so much his associations to the symbols or the choice of symbol-evocative word associations, although some of them led to revealing communication as well, but rather his original choice of the symbols. Both his choice of symbols and his symbolic depictions in the spontaneously created drawings that followed speak to the power of image and symbol in the therapeutic endeavor.

A fifteen-year-old boy, who had suffered enormous emotional pain due to his socially inappropriate behavior and consequent taunting and harassment from his peer group, showed unusual emotional sensitivity in his response to the relational strategy #3 on the SATS. On the word stimulus of "Family" he placed a plum-colored heart, a white heart, a blue heart, and a black heart. On inquiry, he gave the following explanation for his choices, "Family is where all hearts come together, and their hearts are linked to become one." On the word category "Home" he placed a hut with a heart inside it. He explained on inquiry, "Home is a place of refuge, where your heart belongs." I was deeply moved by this teen's responses and on reflection I could more than ever appreciate the injuries to his spirit. He is not only a very intelligent young man who is quite aware of his social ineptness and sometimes inappropriate behaviors, his inability to make conversations with peers, his inability to appreciate the humor of his peers or make jokes that his fellow students would find funny, but on a deep emotional level, he is also an extremely caring and feeling young man who values and appreciates the love of his family and longs for connection with peers.

Another quite touching experience occurred when doing the SATS relational strategy with an eleven-year-old girl who has experienced a series of profound losses, the most devastating of which was abandonment by her father when she was four years old. She has not seen him since. On the word category "Family" she placed symbols representing mother and child and explained, "This is my family." On the word category "Mother" she placed four blue hearts. On inquiry, she stated, "Because I really love my mother." On the word category "Father" she originally left it blank. Then she placed a black heart. She said, "The black heart stands for evil." Then she took the black heart off and instead placed a small pink heart. She said, "I've changed my mind again because I still love him. It is a small heart but I do still love him." I was deeply moved as once again a child expressed love, loyalty, and longing for a parent who has not been able to parent. The capacity for love and forgiveness in children is incredible to witness.

Another fifteen-year-old boy, on the SATS strategy #1 put a white heart on the evocative word stimulus "Hugs." He explained that hugs can make your heart feel better and grow stronger. This opened up an important discussion about his longing for more displays of affection in his family, not only toward him, but between his parents, something that had been absent for as long as he could remember. The lack of emotional connection within his family was a factor in his depression. His ability to talk about the feelings of loneliness and disconnection that he secretly suffered for a long time was a contributing factor to reducing those barriers of isolation and relieving the depression.

An eleven-year-old girl when doing the SATS strategy #1, placed a man in a guard uniform on the evocative word stimulus "Weak." She explained that he looks like he has turned to the "dark side" because he has a mean look on his face. His weakness was manifested by his inability to resist the temptation to turn to the dark side. This led into an important discussion about trust and betrayal. These issues were of utmost importance to her because at an earlier age she had been molested by her grandfather.

As a result of this therapeutic exchange she was not only able to discuss the hurt and rage she experienced when betrayed by her grandfather but led to an important series of discussions about how she could decide who is to be trusted and who is not. She was able to appreciate that she is in a better position now that she is older to pick up on signs that someone is not worthy of trust. We focused on what signs she would look for that would tell her this. The effects of these discussions were to empower her, so that she could appreciate that she was no longer vulnerable to someone exploiting her in the way she was as a little girl. It also led to some very important exchanges in the therapy about the possibility of overinterpreting danger, which is common in trauma victims, and what signs could she look for that would tell her that a person is worthy of trust. This ability to discriminate is vital for trauma victims, otherwise they may judge in a hasty manner that someone who might be helpful to them is untrustworthy.

This child also affirmed the power of symbols when she placed on the evocative word "Pain" two halves of a heart. She then stated, "True pain is when your heart is broken—the pain is more than the pain of wounded soldiers." Only a child who had suffered such a devastating betrayal would be able to describe the pain with such vivid language. It is possible that this therapeutic exchange would eventually have taken place without the use of the SATS but it moved the therapy to a deeper, more heartfelt place sooner rather than later.

Still another important door was opened in therapy with a twelve-year-old boy who suffered social rejection on a chronic basis due to his developmental oddities in spite of his high intelligence. On the evocative word stimulus "Death" he placed a symbol of a tombstone. He then explained, "When you cease to exist—someone that nobody cares about anymore—someone completely forgotten even if still alive." This youngster's social experience was worse than the pain of death—far worse. To feel that you cease to exist, that nobody cares about you anymore, and that you are completely forgotten even if still alive, that would be a fate worse than death. His ability to share the depths of his anguish and despair about his lack of inclusion and belonging both socially and within his family was an important step forward—reducing his sense of isolation and loneliness.

ADDITIONAL CLINICAL APPLICATIONS

Hearts-Only Strategy

In the "Hearts-Only" strategy children are instructed to use only the heart-shape symbols and place them on the relational domain boards in whatever way they choose. They can put more than one heart on any of the relational word categories or if they choose they can put none on one or more categories. Their choices would then be explored in depth. For the purposes of this strategy, it is useful to have a variety of hearts of different colors and sizes to choose from.

Home/Family Only Relational Strategy

In this variation of the relational domain strategy only the word categories "Home" and "Family" are used. The child is instructed to pick one symbol from the entire collection to represent the "Home" and another symbol for "Family" before a specific emotionally significant event occurred such as parents separating, brother or sister leaving for college, a family member dying, or a family member going to jail. After the children choose the symbols and explain their choices, they are then asked to choose a symbol to represent the family and another symbol for home after the event occurred. Once again, the reasons behind the choices are explored. Finally, the child is asked to pick a symbol to represent the family as he or she would like it to be in the future and the choice of symbol once again becomes the focus of a give-and-take dialogue with the therapist. While it may be too abstract for some youngsters, it may be helpful particularly with pre-teens and adolescents to ask them to select a symbol that would represent the steps that would enable the family and home to become more like they want it to be.

Parents-Only Relational Strategy

Another variation is to use just the "Mother" and "Father" stimulus words from the relational domains and ask the child to pick a symbol to represent each parent before an event with significant emotional impact on the family occurred, such as, "When Dad starting drinking again" or "When mom was diagnosed" or "When your sister had her accident." Then the child can be asked to pick a symbol for each parent after this emotionally significant event occurred and finally, depending on the child and whether they are capable of a more abstract task, the therapist can conclude with asking the child to pick a symbol for each parent depicting how they would like them to be in the future. The rationale behind this and the above "Home" and "Family" strategy is that when a traumatic event occurs in the family, typically there is a longing shared by the family members "to turn the clock back" to the time in the family's life before the devastating event. By enlisting the power of symbols and images in this process, the child may be able to capture the feelings related to the impact of these significant emotional events in the family that words are often inadequate or unavailable to tell.

If this is productive for the child it could be expanded to include siblings by bringing in the "Brother" and "Sister" domain board. The client can be instructed to pick a symbol for each brother and/or sister and then proceed as described above.

Self-Only Relational Strategy

Another variation of the above strategy is to use the "Self" category from the relational domain boards and instruct the client to pick a symbol for "Self" prior to the occurrence of a major emotional event, a symbol for "Self" after the event, and a symbol for "Self" depicting a vision for "Self" in the future.

Working with Countertransference in Supervision

The specific application that I have developed to deal with countertransference issues and other issues in supervision entails the use of a symbol-sorting task with the following word categories:

The four word categories are included in the SATS Clinical Manual (Crenshaw, in press b) and placed in front of the supervisee. The supervisee is then invited to select from the collection of miniatures the symbols they wish to place on each of the categories representing their work with a particular child, family, and supervisor, as well as selecting one or more symbols to represent the self as therapist.

When the supervisee has accomplished the symbol-sorting task above, it is laid out in front of both the supervisor and supervisee and together in a collaborative process they can pursue the meaning it has for that particular supervisee. The supervisees can use this same tool to self-monitor and self-

```
┌─────────────────────────────┐
│                             │
│          CHILD              │
│                             │
└─────────────────────────────┘


┌─────────────────────────────┐
│                             │
│          FAMILY             │
│                             │
└─────────────────────────────┘


┌─────────────────────────────┐
│                             │
│         THERAPIST           │
│                             │
└─────────────────────────────┘


┌─────────────────────────────┐
│                             │
│        SUPERVISOR           │
│                             │
└─────────────────────────────┘
```

Textbox   3.1.   Child-Family-Therapist-Supervisor

examine their reactions with any of their on-going therapy cases if they so choose.

DISCUSSION

The use of symbols is one of a number of ways that children can tell their story. Jung (1961) stated, "The patient who comes to us has a story that is not told, and which as a rule, no one knows of. To my mind, therapy only begins after the investigation of the whole personal story. It is the patient's secret, the rock against which he is shattered. And, if I know his secret story, I have the key to his treatment" (p. 117). In attempting to understand the story told through symbols, I approach the task as taught by Bonime (1962, 1989) from a Culturalist Psychoanalytic framework. There are no preconceived notions, no assumed meanings, and no universal or cookbook glossary but rather the therapist explores the significance of the symbol for this particular client at this particular time and place. Erskine (2001) explained, "When clients reveal dreams, we do not argue about the dream's symbols representation of reality or whether these symbols can be proven by research. Rather, we examine the meaning of the dream in the context of the client's life experience" (p. 135).

Rollo May (1975) defined symbol "as that which draws together and unites experience" (p. 703). May further explained, "As long as there is unconscious material expressing itself in poetry, dreams, experiences of ecstasy, imagination (i.e., as long as we are human), symbols will be necessary to carry the richer and deeper meaning that cannot be communicated by operational language" (p. 704).

The therapeutic value of symbols was articulated by Bonime (1962) when he discussed dream symbols. He stated, "The distinguishing quality of dream symbols is their semantic specificity. They present themselves with exquisite individuality, arising out of the core of the patient's uniquely personal history and offering cognitive and emotional definitions of a specific plexus of his experience. They convey meaning with a vividness that would be impossible to achieve in verbal terms" (p. 31). Bonime cautioned against assuming universal meanings of symbols. He explained, "When a universal dictionary of symbols is mechanically applied, therapists may be seriously misled. They may miss, for any particular patient, the unique significance of his symbols. One avoids this pitfall, when dealing with dreams or other material, by deriving from the individual himself the meaning of the data coming from him" (pp. 33–34).

HOW THESE STRATEGIES CAN
ENHANCE THE THERAPY PROCESS

The SATS are strategies intended to initiate heart-to-heart therapeutic dialogue about matters that are emotionally meaningful that a significant portion of youngsters will not readily engage in without facilitation. The symbol strategies may be particularly useful for children who are unaware of the sources of their inner pain. The associative activity allows for rich clinical data that will allow therapists to gather hypotheses about what is causing hurt when the child doesn't know. Some of these hypotheses will be discarded as more data is gathered and consistent themes and patterns emerge that enable the therapist to better understand both the child's inner life and relational world. Some of the therapeutic conversations that need to take place are difficult to initiate by the child because of the sensitive nature of the content. These strategies include structured activities, symbol, and artistic depiction that often lead to the sensitive place, the part of the child's heart that is hurting the most, and when that most vulnerable spot is touched in an empathic manner the therapy process is furthered.

RESOURCES FOR CLINICIANS OF
MATERIALS DESCRIBED IN THIS CHAPTER

The Symbol Association Therapy (SATS) Clinical Manual can be ordered from Jason Aronson/Rowman & Littlefield Publishers (www.rowmanlittle-field.com/AronsonP/); 800) 462-6420. The SATS Clinical Manual contains the evocative word stimulus sheets for the various SATS strategies and recording sheets for the strategies.

The SATS Basic Symbol Kit can be obtained from The Self Esteem Shop (www.selfesteemshop.com/); (800) 251-8336.

• 4 •

Building the Therapeutic
Alliance by Honoring Strengths

𝒫urpose: In this chapter the strategies are designed to highlight and honor the strengths of children and their families, particularly their courage, determination, and perseverance when faced with difficult challenges. Therapists strengthen the therapeutic alliance when they recognize and validate the fighting spirit of children. The therapy process is also enhanced by honoring the resources within the family, because these are the supports the child will draw on long after the therapy has ended.

"UNSUNG HEROES AND HEROINES"
(STRATEGIES FOR CHILDREN AGES 6 TO 17)

The Story

"A man was working on his car in his garage when he heard a loud screech of tires and a crash nearby. He ran out and saw a truck turned over along the highway behind his house. The man—who was married and had two young sons—raced up the hill, scaled a fence, and by the time he reached the over-turned semi-trailer truck it was on fire. The fire was rapidly approaching the cab where the driver was trapped. The man, without any hesitation, kicked out the windshield and pulled the frightened man from the burning truck. The man in the truck had minor cuts and burns but otherwise was okay. The man who rescued him was more severely cut and badly burned on his arms. The man who saved the other man's life never saw the man he rescued again. There were no newspaper articles written about his daring rescue. He never received any awards or medals, few people except for his family ever heard the story, but he was truly courageous and heroic, an unsung hero."

Follow-Up

1. There are many unsung heroes and heroines in the world who are never recognized or honored but heroes and heroines all the same. Can you name some that you know or have heard about?
2. Is there some way that you could be considered a courageous, unsung hero or heroine?
3. Is there a member of your family or a friend or someone that you know well that could be considered an unsung hero or heroine?
4. What can we learn from these unrecognized acts of courage?
5. Tell me about a time when you faced something difficult with courage and determination.
6. Who else knows about your courage and determination?
7. Who is the most courageous person you know?
8. Do you believe that a courageous and determined person never asks for help?
9. When are there good reasons for asking others to help?
10. Do you think it is okay for boys to cry?
11. Do you think it is okay for girls to cry?
12. Do you think it is okay for grown-ups to cry?

Drawing Directives

Some children may wish to draw their unsung heroes and heroines. The drawn images of their personal heroes and heroines may enable them to expand further on their relationships and feelings regarding these respected people in their lives.

Symbol Work with "Unsung Heroes or Heroines"

Children can be asked to pick the symbols that they feel would best represent the unsung heroes or heroines from a collection of miniatures. The therapist can expand the therapeutic dialogue by pursuing the child's choice of symbols in each case.

Discussion

Unsung Family Heroes and Heroines   Stories of courage and determination can be inspiring but it is important that kids be helped to recognize that courage and determination can take many forms. Compared to the tales of heroic courage that make some people famous there are acts of courage that are not recognized and honored by others. My late father was one of my "unsung heroes." Though he rarely spoke of it, he was the one who rescued the man from the burning truck.

It is important to pursue with children their own family unsung heroes and heroines. Often it is helpful to do this in a family session because children may be hearing these stories from their parents for the first time. But stories of family heroism, even unsung heroism, can be source of positive identity and pride for children.

An eight-year-old boy drew a picture of his father. He stated, "My dad is my unsung hero. He is always there when I need him. He makes me feel safe and I know I can always count on him no matter what. But I don't think he gets enough credit for being a good dad." This child's comments are deeply touching because he honors his father for being a good dad and appreciates all that his father does for him.

I used to love to hear family stories and would persuade my grandparents to tell my favorites over and over again. During the time of the Civil War, my great-great uncle Dr. Tom Allen traveled by horse and buggy to make house calls to administer to the sick and to deliver babies. My mother and uncle remember Dr. Tom's office in a small building on the Allen family farm where they grew up. Uncle Tom would make his house calls sometimes in the middle of night and in some cases involving delivery of babies or when people were acutely ill he would remain by the bedside ministering to his patients through the night. My uncle recently gave me the log kept by Dr. Tom of his house calls, and I found it fascinating that the usual charge for these house calls was 25 cents or in some cases as much as 50 cents. In many cases, his patients could not pay the charge and he delivered the highly personal care for free. Others paid over time. Uncle Tom died at age twenty-nine of pneumonia long before the age of antibiotics.

Fast forward from the 1860s when health care, although primitive by today's standards, was delivered in a highly personal and humanistic manner, to 2006, when on a winter night I came out of my office at 6:00 p.m. to find an older man laying on the concrete parking lot. I called 911 and put blankets around him and a pillow under his head. He was having symptoms suggestive of a stroke but he begged me not to call the ambulance because he had no health insurance. All the while as we waited for the ambulance to arrive the man kept pleading with me to cancel the call because he could not pay for the care he would need. Has the heart completely gone out of our health care system?

While Uncle Tom was making his house calls during the 1860s, my great-grandfather, James (Jimmy) Allen, Tom's brother, served as an infantry soldier for the Union Army. My great-great grandparents David and Lavina

Allen became a part of the underground slave railroad. My mother, her brother, and sister used to play in the attic with a secret compartment where the slaves were hidden. I am proud to be the namesake of David Allen. Lavina Allen's mother was a Native American.

Jimmy and Elizabeth Allen, my great-grandparents, followed in the tradition of Jimmy's parents, David and Lavina, and opened their home to many who needed temporary and long-term shelter, including a girl they raised who I came to know as "Aunt Ida." In addition, they took in a number of others in need including two African American women, one of whom had been deserted by her husband, was quite ill, and needed a home. They nursed her back to health and helped her eventually to find a home. The other had been a slave in a wealthy family in the area by the name of Holton (fictitious name). Slaves often took the name of their owners and so Dicey Holton continued to work for the Holton family until she was too ill to be productive. Although the Holton family had taught her to read and write and apparently treated her well as long as she was able to work, when she became feeble they dismissed her. Homeless, she appeared at the door of Jimmy and Elizabeth Allen where she was taken in and lived the remaining fifteen years of her life. When she died, my great-grandparents tried to bury her in the family plot behind the Corinth Church near their farm. They were denied permission, however, and were required to bury her in a cemetery in a town nine miles away that was reserved for black people. They took her body on the back of a horse-drawn wagon to bury her in that cemetery since no undertaker in the community at that time was willing to handle the arrangements for a black person.

Among others that Jimmy and Elizabeth Allen took into their home was a German immigrant by the name of Mr. Harshberger. At the time, he was facing hard times and he remained with my great-grandparents until he was able to accumulate enough money to find his own place. Mr. Harshberger eventually opened his own store in the nearest town of Foley, Missouri. Jimmy Allen was told he could have all the credit he wanted to buy things from the store because Mr. Hershberger never forgot what Jimmy and Elizabeth Allen did for him when he was down and out.

Another man who was desperately poor stayed with the Allen family for quite a lengthy period until he was able to get on his feet. He went away to work and then many years later he became ill and he returned to the Allen family and greeted them by saying, "I have come home to die." And so he did a short time later.

I am grateful for the examples of my grandparents of two and three generations prior of opening their hearts and homes to those who were oppressed and downtrodden. I have a letter given to me by my uncle that was written by

Dicey Holton, the former slave, to my great grandparents. I treasure it and hope to pass it on to my grandchildren as a reminder of the difference that genuine caring and humanity can make. My great-grandparents too are my unsung family heroes.

The questions in follow-up about whether it is okay for boys, girls, and grown-ups to cry are suggested to give opportunities for the therapist to challenge any maladaptive beliefs that being heroic or courageous means you never feel fear, sadness, or vulnerability. Such beliefs would interfere with self-acceptance as well as reaching out to others for help when needed.

Courageous Children Getting out of bed in the morning is an act of courage for a school-phobic child or a depressed youngster. Boyd and Ross (1994) described the "courage tapes," which consisted of videotaped interviews with children. The tapes were about thirty minutes long and were structured around questions requiring the children to describe how they had used courage to overcome problems and what advice they would give others who are coping with similar problems. This approach offers great potential for highlighting the courage and determination of kids. The children can be given a copy of the tape to keep. I find this technique not only highlights the courage of children, but in my experience they welcome the opportunity to share their experience in order to help others. One of the children I videotaped for the "courage tapes" described how he struggled with dyslexia but continues to work hard and is now holding his own in a demanding academic program. Another adolescent described how she coped with the suicide of a family member and more recently helped a friend who was experiencing depression and suicidal thoughts. In each instance the children are pleased that these tapes might help others faced with similar situations.

Usually these small acts of courage and determination would "fly under the radar" of both the child and the family, but it is crucial that they do not escape the notice of the therapist. The clinician can make a valuable contribution by alerting the family and child to look for and honor these everyday acts of courage and fighting spirit.

Courage and Determination Are Needed in Therapy Courage and determination are also required, but often unrecognized, on the part of both the child and therapist in order to achieve change and growth. For years I enjoyed climbing mountains with friends mostly in the Catskills but once in the Adirondacks. I quickly learned that only part of the challenge was physical; a major portion was mental. I remember climbing Giant Mountain in the Adirondacks with my brother-in-law, John. We encountered five "false peaks" during the long and difficult climb and had close encounters with rattlesnakes. In other words, five times we thought we saw the peak—the end to our long and tough climb—only to be mistaken. When we climbed higher we noticed another peak behind the one we thought was the top. Each time this happened our heart sank; it was hot, and we were weary and frustrated. Each time it was tempting to say, "That's enough, let's turn back." But each time we did the mental work required to lift our spirits, combat our demoralization, to remind ourselves that although our legs were tired, we could keep going, we could do this, and we would reach the peak. And we did; it was a rewarding sense of accomplishment when we finally reached the summit and enjoyed the commanding view only available from the top.

In therapy with children "false peaks" are not uncommon. Both the child and therapist may feel tempted to turn back; the climb may seem too difficult, the obstacles too great, but courage, perseverance, and determination at those very moments when you feel most defeated may pay rich emotional dividends for both the child and clinician. Some children are masters at convincing would-be helpers to give up on them. Then the child is relieved of the necessity of change, which is a scary process. At those times it is easy to mistake a "false peak" for the real top. The therapist is relieved because they need not continue the uphill and sometimes scary climb. It takes clinical courage and determination to stay the course to address in an adequate way the invisible wounds and injuries of children. Short cuts or quick fixes are often "false peaks."

If the child has shown unusual courage in the course of therapy in facing and overcoming a difficult or painful issue, the therapist could identify the child as an unsung hero or heroine. The child could be asked, in this instance, to draw a picture of self to add to the collection of everyday heroes or heroines. I always invite the child to take the pictures with them, after I seek permission to scan the pictures so I have a cumulative record of the drawings. Some children, however, prefer that I keep the originals, in which case I offer the total collection back to them at the end of therapy as part of the termination process. They then have a serial set of drawings spanning the course of therapy.

"PATSY ANNE"
(A STRATEGY FOR CHILDREN AGES 6 TO 12)

Purpose: *This strategy is designed to inspire children to believe in themselves even if they have significant obstacles to overcome. Children may become demoralized and discouraged because, as Rudolph Driekurs pointed out many years ago, children who need encouragement the most typically receive it the least.*

The Story

"In Juneau, Alaska, the capital of that huge and beautiful state, right on the dock where people get off of cruise ships to go ashore is a statue of Patsy Anne, a dog who years ago won the hearts of the people of this small city as well as the tourists arriving on the ships. Patsy Anne hung out on the docks because she loved to meet the ships and the passengers upon their arrival. She always seemed somehow to know before anyone else when a ship was about to arrive and she also somehow knew at which dock the ship would be moored.

"This was quite remarkable because Patsy Anne had been deaf since birth. When Patsy Anne's owner died, she was adopted by a group of Longshoremen who had living quarters downtown near the docks. When Patsy Anne died the community that loved her and the repeat visitors who enjoyed her friendly greetings all pitched in to raise money for a sculptured likeness of Patsy Anne that is beautiful and seen immediately by visitors when they disembark the ships. In a way, Patsy Anne is still at her place on the dock greeting visitors in her special, warm, and friendly way."

Storytelling Directives

"Now please tell a story about a pet, one that you have known or heard or read about that has inspired you—a pet that showed courage and determination in coping with a difficult situation."

Follow-Up to the Story

1. What inspired you the most about the pet in your story?
2. What can be learned from your story?
3. Since no one is perfect, except for brief moments like when you get a 100 on a Math test, it could be said that we are all challenged in one way or another. We can be good in Spelling, but not so good in Math, for example. Name a challenge or an obstacle you have faced.
4. What has helped you the most in coping with this challenge?
5. Pretend that you were invited to speak to a group of kids on the topic, "Never Give Up." What would be the main points that you would make?
6. Suppose you were invited to give a talk to a group of kids titled "My Five Best Coping Strategies." What would those five best coping strategies be?

Drawing Strategy

Some children may wish to expand on this strategy by drawing their heroic pet(s) that they have known that overcame obstacles in their lives. The therapeutic conversation can be greatly extended by collaborative exploration of the drawings.

Symbol Work with "Patsy Anne"

Children can be asked to pick a symbol to represent Patsy Anne and any pets that they have known that faced and overcame obstacles including the pet(s) in the stories they create. Alternatively, children can be asked to pick a symbol for each pet that was special to them in some way and explore their choices of symbols and the feelings underlying those picks.

Discussion

Pets play an important role in the lives of many children. Stories of heroic pets can segue into discussing their own acts of courage and determination in facing adversity in their lives. In addition, children become significantly attached to their pets and their death can be a significant loss for them. Along with the death of a grandparent, the death of a pet is frequently one of their earliest encounters with the death of someone special and important to them. Adults sometimes minimize the death of pets, regarding them simply as "critters." For children, however, it can be very important, and they tend to regard pets, along with many adults, as members of the family. This strategy allows for exploration of feelings among children regarding special pets that have died for whom they have not adequately grieved.

"STANDING OVATION"
(STRATEGY FOR CHILDREN AGES 9 TO 17)

Purpose: *Consistent with the strengths-based approach, this strategy creates another opportunity to identify, highlight, and reinforce important abilities, talents, and strengths in the older child, pre-teen and adolescent that they may not recognize or give proper emphasis.*

Directives

"One of the most dramatic honors anyone can receive is a standing ovation from an auditorium or stadium full of people. Let's pretend that you are being presented an award and as you walk to the front to receive your award, you receive a standing ovation. Try to hear the applause and picture yourself walking to the front of the auditorium to receive your award and seeing people all around you standing and clapping in your honor."

Follow-Up

1. What is the award for?
2. What are some of the nice things that were said about you that led the crowd to give you a standing ovation?
3. Have you received any awards so far in your life? If so tell me about them.
4. Not everybody who deserves a standing ovation ever receives one. Have you done something already in your life that you feel deserves a standing ovation?
5. Does anyone in your family or someone else important to you deserve a standing ovation for something they have done, even if they didn't receive one?

Drawing Strategy

The therapeutic dialogue with some children will be significantly expanded by inviting them to draw a picture of the award or of them receiving the award.

Symbol Work with "Standing Ovation"

Children are instructed to pick a symbol to represent each person that they believe deserves a standing ovation. The choice of symbols and the persons selected, including self if chosen, can then be explored to further the therapeutic dialogue with the child.

Discussion

Reinforcing the Therapeutic Alliance by a Competency and Strengths-Based Approach   Robert Brooks (2003) explained that we all adopt certain mindsets in our approach to kids. Some have a pathology-centered mind-set. After becoming disillusioned with that approach, Brooks now adopts the mindset of focusing on hope, strengths and resilience. How do we nurture hope and resilience in kids? Brook's (2003) answer is, "... to provide relationships with kids that touch their minds, hearts and spirits."

The strategies described above are strengths-based and focus children on their competencies and assets. The assets that the client brings to therapy are crucial ingredients common to all effective psychotherapies. In the family therapy field, Waters and Lawrence (1993) wrote about the importance of competence, courage, vision, hope, and strength in the families we work with and seek to help. They encouraged us to move away from an exclusive focus on pathology to attend to the healthy strivings in people for mastery and connection. The approach assumes that people at their core are healthy. Healthy energy is embedded in pathology.

The competence based approach (Waters and Lawrence, 1993) also assumes that human behavior is motivated by: (1) the urge for mastery (based on the work of Robert White, 1959); (2) the urge for connection (consistent with the work of the Stone Center, Miller and Stiver, 1997); and (3) the urge for autonomy. Lawrence (2003) indicated that the competence approach assumes that the highest level of development is individuation with connection.

Minuchin and Colapinto (1994) in a four-day consultation at the Astor Home for Children stated, "If you want to be a diagnostician you will focus on pathology. If you want to be a change agent you will focus on strengths. It is a question of mind-set."

Brooks (1993) urged us to search for what he calls "islands of competence" in the child. As Brooks (2003) stated, "They need to feel they can contribute something to the world; that they can make a difference." Levine (2002), in *A Mind at a Time,* suggested that we look for "buried treasure in children." Hardy and Laszloffy (2005) urged us to look for "badges of ability" in children and families.

Evidence-Base of a Strengths-Based Approach

The strengths/competency-based approach has received increased emphasis in family therapy and the mental health field in general over the last decade (Allison, Stacy, Dadds, Roeger, et al., 2003). It has garnered interest in the juvenile justice system in treating both male and female adolescent offenders (Clark, 1998; Corcoran, 1997; Johnson, 2003; Pepi, 1997; Querimit and Connor, 2003), and in residential treatment and inpatient treatment of children and adolescents (Lietz, 2004; Nickerson, Salamone, Brooks, and Colby, 2004; LeBel, Stomberg, Duckworth, Kerzner, et al., 2004) and in the treatment of children and youth in general (Corcoran, 2005; Helton and Smith, 2004).

Clinical Illustration of the Strengths-Based Approach

An extremely sad and forlorn boy entered the therapy room. Keyshawn, an eleven-year-old boy in residential treatment, had virtually given up. He no longer retained hope that he would return to his family. He was in a downward spiral and increasingly aggressive and violent. He asked whether we would send him to a hospital. I sensed that he was testing us to see if we felt hopeless and ready to give up on him as well. He told me on that occasion that he almost didn't come for his session with me. He said, "When I got up this morning, I didn't feel like getting up, I just wanted to pull the covers over my head." I said to him, "But you made a decision to get up, get dressed, go to school and you were in school all morning. You didn't feel like coming to see me today, but you did. You are working hard in the session to tell me how badly you feel, how hopeless it seems. You are still trying to communicate and share your feelings with me. That tells me that you have inner strength that you are not in touch with right now, but it is there and you are using it even as we speak."

By delineating his exercise of his strengths, I was also seeking to facilitate hope and the appreciation of his courage and perseverance. In addition, I let him know that I was not buying into the hopelessness. One of the major challenges of working with seriously depressed kids is not being engulfed in their hopelessness.

HOW THESE STRATEGIES CAN ENHANCE THE THERAPY PROCESS

"Pouncing on pathology" and "documenting damage" are too often overlearned habits of mental health professionals. The change process is augmented, however, by focusing on assets, resources, talents, and strengths in children and within their relational network. The techniques detailed in this chapter put the spotlight on these crucial factors in the change equation.

In addition to highlighting the internal and external resources for change, thus making these strengths more consciously accessible, these techniques can foster hope and combat demoralization, one of the cornerstone goals of psychotherapy. If we "pounce on pathology" and "document damage" day after day it will be hard to resist the pull into the demoralization and hopelessness that can be overwhelming to well-intended workers in this field. If we are passionate about delineating strengths, inner resources, healthy functioning, and incremental positive changes, that exist alongside the pathology, we will find plenty to sustain our hope. It all depends on where we put the punctuation!

· 5 ·

Strategies to Strengthen the Self-Observer

*O*verview: *Recent neurobiological research (Siegel, 2007) has validated the work of therapists who recognized the importance of developing in youth a capacity for self-reflection, self-observation, and self-awareness as critical skills in self-regulation as well as social competence. The stories in this chapter are designed to stimulate the capacity for self-observation and to "tickle" or stimulate the curiosity of children in understanding and exploring their own mental processes.*

"THE WISE OLE OWL SPEAKS"
(STRATEGY FOR CHILDREN AGES 9 TO 17)

Purpose: *This story focuses on the key issues of seeking meaning and finding perspective in relation to significant life events. The ability to find meaning and purpose in adverse life events has been found to be important in coping with trauma and in developing resilience to stress. Because of the abstract nature of meaning, this story is unlikely to be useful to children under the age of nine, although there will always be some exceptions.*

The Story

"It was known far and wide among all the animals of the land that one very wise owl liked to perch in the old oak tree near Lake Insight. The word passed quickly among the animals when the Wise Ole Owl was spotted in the tall, strong, and proud oak tree near Lake Insight. The animals of the land in whatever language they spoke—pig, cow, horse, rabbit, squirrel, skunk and so on—were often overheard saying, 'I wish I could think like the Wise Ole

Owl,' or 'I wish I could make good choices and make good decisions like the Wise Ole Owl,' or 'I wish I was as wise and understanding as the Wise Ole Owl.' A goat was overheard saying, 'My life would be so different if I had the knowledge and wisdom of the Wise Ole Owl.' The skunk said, 'Me too.'"

"One summer night, when the moon was full, word was passed first from the chipmunks to the squirrels, from the squirrels to the rabbits, from the rabbits to the goats, from the goats to the cows, from the cows to the horses, and so on, that the Wise Ole Owl was perched in the old oak tree near Lake Insight. All the animals moved as quickly as they could toward the lake, the rabbits and squirrels were well out in front, with the horses in the middle, and the much slower animals, like the pigs and cows, bringing up the rear. The Wise Ole Owl knew that each animal would have to reach Lake Insight at the pace that was right for him or her. The Wise Ole Owl was understanding and patient and urged the other animals to be patient as well, because those who arrived first were getting restless and frustrated. They had been there for some time, but there was still no sign of the pigs and cows.

"Finally, all the animals had arrived, but in spite of the understanding and compassion expressed by the Wise Ole Owl, some of the animals made dirty faces at the pigs and cows. There was some mumbling and one of the horses was heard to say to the pigs, 'What took you so long, did you stop and have a picnic along the way?' All the animals laughed, except the pigs and cows. The Wise Ole Owl said, 'The animals who arrived first should show understanding and compassion toward those who arrived last.'"

"The Wise Ole Owl explained, 'Being the one to arrive first is not always the most important thing. Suppose the pigs and cows did stop to have a picnic along the way, after all it is a beautiful night. Basking in the light of the full moon, a picnic would taste very good after a long journey. Maybe the pigs and cows discovered something that the rest of you have yet to learn.' The other animals began to think about what the Wise Ole Owl said and they started to realize they were hungry too, but hadn't even considered stopping along the way. They suddenly realized that if they had not rushed to get here, they might not be so exhausted. The animals turned around and began to see the pigs and cows in a new and more positive way. It may take them longer, but they still arrived at the same place, and they had a more comfortable journey.

"The eager animals could wait no longer, and finally the Stallion blurted out, in horse language, the question to which they all were seeking an answer. He asked the Wise Ole Owl, 'How do we find wisdom and understanding?' All the animals were suddenly very quiet. There was a calm and peaceful stillness around the lake and under the tall and strong oak tree. The Wise Ole Owl paused briefly and then, in a calm but strong voice, said, 'The answer will be found deep within each of you and it will be different for each of you.' The animals couldn't believe what the Wise Ole Owl said. They shook their heads and looked at each other confused and distressed.

"The Wise Ole Owl continued, 'Each of you has a story to tell, a story about the life you have lived, in that story are all the lessons that you need to learn. And if you learn them well, you too will be wise and understanding. I want each of you to go home. When you have learned your lessons well, I want you to come back here one at a time and tell me your story but don't come back until you have learned the lessons contained in the story of your life.'"

Storytelling Directives

Each child is instructed to pick one of the animals to come back to Lake Insight and tell the story of the lessons they have learned from their life to the Wise Ole Owl. "Now the Wise Ole Owl sees that the (name of animal) has arrived and is ready to tell the story. The Wise Ole Owl says, 'I am happy for you that you have learned important lessons in life and that you have reached a point of self-understanding, compassion, and wisdom that you are ready to tell me your story. You may start now and I will be listening carefully." The child begins.

Follow-Up to the Story

Not all children are able to formulate a complete or well-integrated story of how the animal learns the lessons of life and arrives at self-understanding, wisdom, and compassion. Nevertheless, therapists should reinforce any steps, no matter how small, taken by the child toward this goal. If the child completely draws a blank at storytelling, go back to the drawing and use it to stimulate some dialogue. If the child chose a rabbit, for example, you could ask relational questions such as "Did the rabbit figure things out all alone or did the rabbit ask the other animals to help?" "How did the rabbit know that he was ready to tell his story?" "Did the rabbit tell his story to anyone else before going to the Wise Ole Owl?"

The Wise Ole Owl puppet has been a pivotal character in the puppet play of the resistant and guarded children I have treated. I often suggest to children that because the Wise Ole Owl has been around a long time, and because he is wise, that he may be able to offer some wisdom and helpful advice. He can represent the voice of reason, the child's better judgment, or the conscience or super-ego. Many impulsive, action-oriented children don't learn from their mistakes nor do they respond to punishment. They don't learn to reflect, to consult their conscience, or to appeal to their better judgment. This storytelling strategy requires them to think, reflect, and consider the important lessons they have learned from their life experience.

If children seem stumped because the task appears too abstract for them, I may say to them, "Sometimes we learn lessons in life the hard way. We can listen to the wise, experienced adults in our lives, our parents, our teachers, and our grandparents who try to guide us and keep us from making painful mistakes. Even though they mean well, we sometimes don't listen and we learn lessons the hard way, often in a painful way. Think of some lessons you have learned the hard way and tell me about them when you are ready."

Brandon's Story (age 9)   "The pig said to the Wise Ole Owl, 'One important lesson I learned is to love my little brother. When he was born I hated him. I used to be so mad at him because he always got what he wanted and I never got what I wanted. I looked for chances to get even with him. I would not let him play with my toys and when mom wasn't watching I would push him down. I now love my brother and I think he is kind of cool."

Discussion

Fascinating is that Brandon's story suggests that his intense sibling rivalry is resolved when, in fact, he is still struggling with this issue. Brandon has stopped his violence toward his younger brother and that is a major breakthrough, but he still harbors intense resentment and sharing with his younger sibling is not his strong suit. By portraying the issue as resolved, a degree of hopefulness is suggested; he can achieve a solution and he has a map of what that solution would be like in his mind.

Also intriguing is that Brandon, with his unusually intense rivalry issue with his younger sibling, picked "the pig" as the animal to identify with and to tell their story to the Wise Ole Owl. This may suggest some awareness of his self-centeredness and corresponding guilt. This, too, is regarded as a healthy and positive sign. Research by Tangney and Dearing (2002) reveals that guilt is largely a healthy and constructive emotion that involves condemnation of specific action(s). Shame, on the other hand, is a destructive emotion and involves condemnation of self.

Further exploration with Brandon revealed that he experienced appropriate guilt and that his feelings didn't cross the line into shame. If shame-based, then I would have challenged his condemnation of self. Instead, I simply validated his guilt, "It feels bad to hurt your little brother."

As therapists, we can help children to take responsibility for the specific actions for which they should rightly feel guilt, but dispute vigorously their shamed-based views of self. This was partially accomplished by helping Bran-

Drawing 5.1. "The Pig Tells His Story to the Wise Ole Owl"

don solve the problem of his maltreatment of his little brother, but also by focusing on his strengths, positive actions, and qualities, and by validating what
he has to give (Crenshaw & Hardy, 2005). Hardy stated in a personal communication (August, 2003), "When we validate what children have to give,

we elevate their spirit; if they feel they have nothing to give, nothing to contribute, it punctures their spirit."

When a child is engaged in intense sibling rivalry, I have found it helpful to ask the question, at least in my mind, "What is it that this child has that is just his or her own?" Sometimes a powerful antidote is to encourage each parent to spend some undivided, one-on-one time with each child at least once a week. The results can be magical. Parents may argue that finding an hour block of time each week is unrealistic. But when you ask how much time is spent trying to intervene in the acrimonious battles between the siblings, the parents may view this commitment as an attractive trade-off and well worth the investment of their time.

Rivalry issues intensify when the supplies are limited due to the pressures on families, especially in today's world where economic pressures require in most families that both parents be employed outside the home. At the end of the day, family members can return home seeking healing and repair from the bruises they sustained during the day, or at the other end of the continuum, they return home anxious to share with interested family members the highlights and successes of their day. It is a commentary on the fast-paced, Internet speed conditions of economic and social life in our contemporary world that parents often are exhausted at the end of their long and busy work day and may struggle to find the energy to listen in an attentive way to either the stories of bruises or successes in the child's day.

It is also not uncommon that parents have little time to listen to each other. We need to multiply by an unknown but significant factor these pressures for a single parent struggling to make things work economically for the family and also to meet the myriad emotional needs of the children. I wish to emphasize, however, that in my experience, the majority of parents do the best that they can to meet these multiple, complex, and sometimes conflicting needs of their families. They have my utmost and profound respect.

Symbolic Play with the Wise Ole Owl

The above story could be dramatized by having the child take the Wise Ole Owl puppet or if the child prefers the other animals and be the voice of either the owl or the other animals as they one at a time come to tell their story about the lessons they have learned. It allows for expansion of the dialogue regardless of which role the therapist is assigned. I always ask the child to decide which role the therapist should play. If the therapist is assigned the role of the other animals, it offers opportunities to share other lessons learned and meaning that arises out of life struggles and suffering. If the therapist is assigned the role of the Wise Ole Owl, it offers opportunities to ask questions of each of the animals who come forth to tell their story, enriching the dialogue around the issue of search for meaning and purpose. Some of the questions that can serve as a sample for many others that a therapist may ask are shown below:

1. How did you decide you were ready to tell your story?
2. Did you learn the lessons of life on your own or did someone help you?
3. Were there other lessons that you learned that might be helpful to someone else?
4. What was the hardest lesson you learned?
5. What lessons have you learned that you would want to pass on to your baby animals?
6. If you were to write the lessons you learned in the form of a story, what title would you give your story?
7. Do you think lessons always have to be learned the hard way?
8. Do you think it is important to respect your elders?
9. Whom in your family did you learn the most from?
10. How will the lessons you have learned change your life from now on?

Symbol Work with the Wise Ole Owl

Some children may prefer the use of symbols to puppets or some may wish to do both. The child is invited to pick a symbol to represent the Wise Ole Owl and each of the animals that comes to tell its story. The child may want to be the voice for each of the symbols and if not, the follow-up would center simply on the reasons for the child choosing a particular symbol for each of the characters in the story. If there has been a wise person in the child's life that they have turned to in times of trouble for advice, the child could be asked to pick a symbol for the wise person and a symbol for self and even to pick a symbol to represent the trouble that led them to seek out advice. These are all options to further the therapeutic exchange in a potentially meaningful way.

"BLOW-UP BERNIE"
(STRATEGY FOR CHILDREN AGES 9 TO 14)

Purpose: *This strategy is intended to explore through the metaphor of storytelling and the symbolic depiction of the child's drawing some of the key issues that children* *who are prone to reactive-impulsive aggression face. This kind of aggressive behavior is typical of children with ADHD or who struggle with other subtle neurodevelopmental deficits. The story is intended to help such children understand the obstacles they face so they can develop not only greater self-awareness but self-empathy as well. Another objective is to create hope that they can learn to manage their aggressive impulses.*

The Story

"Blow-Up Bernie created a stir wherever he went because no one knew when he was going to blow his top. Other kids tried to stay away from him when he was on edge but they couldn't always tell if he was about to lose it. When his temper got the best of him, it was not a pretty sight. One by one he lost his friends and one day he was sitting under a tree all alone, sad, and lonely. He remembered a dream he once had that told him how different his life could be if he learned the secret of controlling his temper instead of his temper controlling him. The dream also contained a warning that some of the things that he would have to change he would not like and the changes that are needed might be too hard for him. Or if he made the changes, even though his life would be different and better in many ways, he might want to go back to the life he had before. Blow-Up Bernie was quite puzzled by this part of the dream. If his life could change for the better, if he could gain control of his temper, if he could make and keep friends, why would he want to go back to the life he had before?"

Drawing Directives

"Now try to get a picture in your mind of Blow-Up Bernie. Is he short or tall? What is he wearing? Where is he in your picture? Is he at home? At school? In the park? Is he alone or is he with others? If with others, who are the other people? Is he happy, sad, angry, feeling lonely, or some other feeling? When you have a picture of Blow-Up Bernie in your mind, please draw as best you can your picture of Blow-Up Bernie."

Follow-Up to the Drawing

1. Tell me about your drawing.
2. What title would you give to your drawing?
3. What is Bernie feeling in your picture?
4. Do you think Bernie has anyone who would stand up for him? If so, who do you think he could turn to?

5. If you could give Bernie some advice, what would you tell him?
6. If Bernie changes, do you think he could get his friends back?

Storytelling Directives

"Now make up a story about how Blow-Up Bernie's life turned out. In the story tell whether he learned to get control of his temper or his temper stayed in control of him. Did the part of the dream that was so upsetting to him come true? Did he make changes and then find some things so hard about those changes, even though his life was better, that he wanted to go back to the way his life used to be? Be sure to give the story an ending; how did it all turn out for Bernie in the long run?"

Follow-Up to the Story

1. What title would you give your story?
2. What can be learned from your story?
3. What makes it so hard to change problem behaviors like Bernie's temper?
4. Are there some things that Bernie wouldn't like if he were successful in changing his behavior and controlling his temper?
5. How do you think Bernie's friends would react if Bernie changed his behavior?
6. How do you think his family would react to such positive changes in Bernie?
7. Who do you think would be most surprised if Bernie were to make these positive changes?
8. Who would be happiest if Bernie were to make these changes?

Discussion

Children are not the only ones who are anxious about change. Change is equally hard for adults. The struggle depicted in Blow-Up Bernie's dream is a universal struggle. Human beings tend to cling to misery because misery is familiar; change brings uncertainty, confusion, and anxiety. Sheldon Kopp (1970) offered a psychoanalytic interpretation of the Wizard of the Oz in a fascinating article. He observed that Dorothy decided to go back to "dusty ole Kansas" because "she preferred the security of misery to the misery of insecurity" (p. 72). Walter Bonime told me in supervision sessions that, "There is no place like home and home is our pathology." To change engenders anxiety because the subjective sense of "me" is threatened; it feels like "not-me" (Bonime,

1989). Olga Silverstein (1987), faculty emeritus of the Ackerman Institute of the Family, described the delicate balance of change versus stability. She maintained that some negative consequences always follow change, although most children and families, including some therapists, don't recognize or acknowledge the possibility of negative consequences, while they can easily articulate the positive consequences.

Blow-Up Bernie was shaken by his dream, especially the part that told him he might want to return to the way things were because change would be too hard for him. Bernie could not figure out why he would want to return to his former life, especially if he could find a way to tame his temper, but the disquieting feeling persisted that there was truth to this notion and he could not shake the idea. This concept can be approached through the metaphors of drawing and storytelling. The therapist can respond to the child's story with the following:

"Suppose Blow-Up Bernie didn't blow up anymore. Let's picture him now with friends; kids now invite him to birthday parties, and he does better at school. His life is different and better in many ways, but is there anything he doesn't like about his new life? Can you think of anything that is different in Bernie's life now that might make him want to go back to his old life, or something that he misses about the way things were before?"

If the child draws a blank, the therapist can respond:

"Well suppose one thing he misses about his old life is a sense of power. In the past the other kids feared him. Now the kids are no longer afraid of him. In fact, he sometimes gets picked on by other kids. Do you think he might want to go back to his old life so he could feel powerful again? What else might he miss about the way his life was before?"

Therapists should make every effort to pursue the negative consequences of change. The child and family are usually baffled by such inquiries and yet these forces, largely outside of awareness, can stop the change process in its tracks. It can be helpful to share an experience of your own or of others that involved the struggle to change and the discovery, upon succeeding, of its unwelcome aspects. For example, a young lady loses a dramatic amount of weight and finds boys, all of a sudden, interested in her. Their sexual interest creates anxiety that she never experienced in the overweight condition. A child who is a low academic achiever makes a dramatic turnaround only to discover that parents and teachers now place higher expectations upon him. Don't be fooled; although not always apparent, the negative consequences of change lurk in the background and need to be brought out of the shadows.

In Drawing 5.1, Bernie is laying flat on his back with a bomb underneath him that explodes in this picture. This drawing is a good example of the kind of drawing often seen in children who have been exposed to violence.

Drawing 5.2.   "Blow-Up Bernie"

They never know when "the bomb" is going to go off and consequently can never feel completely safe. Until this child did this drawing she had not previously been able to find the words to express the constant state of fear that she and her siblings experienced daily. It opened up that discussion and led to immediate changes to establish safety in the home for her and her siblings, which included her violent father leaving the home.

Children's feelings go underground for many reasons, but the overarching principle is that children disguise their feelings or deny them when it is not safe to express them and this is especially true of children growing up in violent homes. A need to hide or disown one's feelings can lead a child to be truly confused about their genuine feelings and even their true sense of self. Children of domestic violence often arrive at my office in what I refer to as a "turbo-charged emotional state" or what van der Kolk (2003) might call a hypervigilant or alarm state. Due to the constant threat of violence that surrounds them, their physiological systems are hyperaroused. It is difficult to do therapy under these conditions, since van der Kolk has explained that higher cortical centers go off-line when the mid-brain and brain stem are in a hyperaroused state. Consequently, I utilize a variety of soothing and calming activities to begin sessions with such children. Some children prefer to calm their hyperarousal by listening together to music that they find relaxing and soothing, others may prefer doing breathing or muscle relaxation exercises together, while still others may prefer to take a walk together or draw. It is important to make these activities collaborative so the child feels they are not alone in confronting their physiologically hyperaroused systems.

Puppet Play with Blow-Up Bernie

For action-oriented kids who can't sit still for a story or a drawing, this story lends itself well to directed puppet play. The child can choose to play the part of Blow-Up Bernie by picking one of the boy puppets, or if the child prefers, the therapist can play Bernie and the child can choose to be one of his friends. The starting point for the puppet play can be centered on Bernie being alone after losing all his friends or at the point that he makes changes. In either case, it will probably be of interest and fun for many kids to start with a demonstration of Blow-Up Bernie's problems of losing control of his anger. If the child takes the role of Bernie, the therapist can, in the character of one of Bernie's friends, explore how Bernie was able to change his behavior and the consequences of those changes in relation to his family and friends. If the play is focused on the point when Bernie lost his friends, the therapist in the role of one of his former friends can explore what went wrong and what he could do to get his friends back.

Symbol Work with Blow-Up Bernie

Children can pick a symbol for Bernie and each of his friends and then the therapist can explore their choices and the meaning represented as a way of expanding the therapeutic dialogue. Another way to approach the symbol work is to ask the child to pick symbols from a group of miniatures to represent Bernie's feelings at different points in the story such as (1) when he would lose his temper frequently; (2) when Bernie lost his friends; (3) at the point when he remembered his dream; (4) after he changes or decides not to change.

"THE MISUNDERSTOOD MOUSE" (CHILDREN AGES 6 TO 9)

Purpose: *This projective drawing and storytelling strategy is intended to set the stage for therapeutic dialogue within the metaphor about depression, pessimistic thinking, negative mood, and the impact of these symptoms on relationships. In addition it invites meaningful exchange about the child's ideas and theories about causation of such chronic unhappiness, again within the metaphor provided by the storytelling, drawing, and the use of symbol.*

The Story

"A long time ago in the outskirts of Bristol, England, there lived a mouse known as the Misunderstood Mouse. He was always pouting and sulking about one thing or another. His biggest complaint was that no one understood him. He often said, 'My life would be so much better if only other mice could understand me.' One day the other mice decided they were fed up with his whining, complaining, sulking, and pouting. They circled around the Misunderstood Mouse and said to him, 'Okay, tell us your story. Why do you feel we don't understand you? What is it that you wish us to understand that would make your life better? We are eager to hear your story, so tell us.'"

Drawing Directives

"Before the Misunderstood Mouse tells his story, imagine what the Misunderstood Mouse looks like: Is he big or small? Is he alone or, if not, who is there with him? Does he look happy? Sad? Mad? Confused? When you have that picture clearly in mind, please draw him as best you can. You may include the other mice and their surroundings if you wish. It is your picture and you can do it anyway you choose. Take your time and draw the Misunderstood Mouse as best you can."

Follow-Up to the Drawing

1. Tell me about your drawing.
2. What title would you give to your drawing?

3. What is the mouse feeling in your drawing?
4. What advice would you give to the Misunderstood Mouse?
5. What do you think the other mice should do about the *Misunderstood Mouse?*
6. Who do you think suffers the most—the Misunderstood Mouse or the other mice?

Storytelling Directives

"Now pretend the mice gather around the Misunderstood Mouse because they are quite annoyed with him. He has been complaining for a long time, but perhaps there is something important about the Misunderstood Mouse's life story that they did not know and that he now is ready to tell them. They are very still now as the Misunderstood Mouse gathers up the courage and begins his story: "My mouse brothers and sisters, there is something you don't know about me, and I want to tell you my story. It all began quite a long time ago . . ."

The child takes it from this point. If further prompting is needed, the therapist can ask questions to help set the scene. Some children will be unable to create stories even with support and encouragement from the therapist. The struggles of the Misunderstood Mouse may be too close to their own issues or remind them of some event that is upsetting. In that case, after encouragement and support have failed, it is best to ask the child to choose another play or fantasy activity. By respecting and honoring the defenses the child relies on and by acknowledging the adaptive value they serve in protecting the child, the therapist makes the treatment setting a safer place.

Follow-Up to the Story

1. What would be a good title for your story?
2. What lessons can be learned from your story?
3. Can you think of any other endings to your story besides the one you gave?
4. How do you think things will change for the *Misunderstood Mouse* after he tells his story?
5. How do you think the other mice will respond to him after he tells the story?
6. Looking back on your story, would there be anything you would like to change or do you like it just the way it is?

This story, along with *The Pig That Didn't Fit,* pulls for one of the more potent themes revealed in the spontaneous symbolic play and artwork of children suffering from insecure attachments. Research has demonstrated that secure attachments early in life can buffer children from the impact of stress in their lives. Conversely, insecure attachments place them at greater risk when faced with adversity in later life. A child suffering from insecure attachments will be made anxious by and very reactive to, separation and loss issues. This story targets the greatest fear, the worst nightmare of children, whether real or imagined, that they are the child in their family that doesn't fit and/or the child in the social group that doesn't belong. These fears are magnified in children suffering from multiple losses or frequent disruptions of early attachment relationships. Such fears are typical in many children in the foster care system.

Aaron's Story (age 9)   "I am a little different from the rest of you. I play kind of weird sometimes. I am an exotic kind of mouse. I only have one or

Drawing 5.3.   "The Misunderstood Mouse"

two friends and I would like to have more. If any of you want to be my friend, it would make me very happy. Thank you."

This is a poignant story by a boy whose absorption in fantasy combined with social eccentricities has made it difficult for him in social situations and left him at times lonely and isolated. This story opened up an important portal of entry that enabled him in subsequent sessions to talk directly about these feelings. Once these feelings were acknowledged it was possible to explore strategies to improve social acceptance.

Ricky's Story (age 11) "The Misunderstood Mouse said you mice have never before taken the time to listen to me, and you don't understand what it is like never to be liked. I have always hated you, but I think you hate me more. You have no idea what it is like to feel that nobody likes you no matter what you do or how hard you try."

Ricky's life story was dominated by a series of profound losses, multiple foster home placements, and exposure to violence, abuse, and trauma. His brief story expressed a strong identification with the Misunderstood Mouse. Like the mouse, he has been in a lifelong quest to feel understood and accepted. He expresses poignantly what it is like to feel that nothing he tries seems to work. The story opened a window to the degree of hopelessness and despair this child was suffering. The therapeutic work with this child partly consisted of validating his feelings of hopelessness and gradually enabling him to see how his anger limits his ability to see his own part in social rejection. In addition, the dialogue that follows was intended to help him see new possibilities while remaining within the metaphor.

> **Therapist:** The Misunderstood Mouse doesn't feel that anyone has ever listened to him until now. It is no wonder that he is so angry. He also sounds very hurt. He doesn't believe anyone could understand how much this has hurt him. What would it take to change the *Misunderstood Mouse's* mind? What would show him that people do care and want to understand how he feels?
>
> **Ricky:** His mind is made up. Nothing will change his mind.
>
> **Therapist:** What if someone made a very determined effort to understand how he feels, really listen to him, would that make any difference?
>
> **Ricky:** It is too late.
>
> **Therapist:** I wonder since the Misunderstood Mouse has made up his mind that it is too late whether he would even recognize that other people care about him.

Sometimes it is possible to challenge entrenched ideas of despair, pessimistic thought patterns along with associated anger, and sometimes rage by putting something out on the table that the therapist doesn't expect a response to. In fact, it may be more helpful if the child doesn't respond overtly but rather sits with the idea for a while and lets it take hold. Immediate responses on the part of children can be a way of discarding the idea as quickly as possible without really examining it in any depth. At times I will make this explicit and say to the child I don't want you to respond to this but rather just think about it for a while. The child may or may not bring the matter up again later in therapy. If not, and the timing and context are appropriate and the child is working within the *Invitational Track*, the therapist can follow it up in later session with the following:

> **Therapist**: Ricky, I have been thinking about your story about the Misunderstood Mouse. I have thought about it a lot and what I am wondering is whether the Mouse would even know, would he be able to see or hear that people are trying to understand him. Maybe when he made up his mind that no one cares, no one listens, no one could ever understand him he stopped caring, stopped listening, and stopped trying to understand others. If that is true, how would he know if someone cared and really wanted to understand him? Maybe he doesn't want to take a chance on being hurt again.
>
> **Ricky**: I guess.
>
> **(Please note:** At this point I decided, based on a stronger therapeutic alliance, to step out of metaphor and discuss these painful feelings directly with Ricky.)
>
> **Therapist**: Ricky, I could be way off the mark here, but I wonder if you have some of those same feelings as the Misunderstood Mouse. Have you decided that no one will listen to you or understand you?
>
> **Ricky**: Well, it's true.
>
> **Therapist**: If you decide it's true will you be able to notice if someone really wants to understand and listen to you? Will you notice if someone cares about you?
>
> **Ricky**: It won't happen.
>
> **Therapist**: How will you know, what signs would you look for just in case somebody does?

Discussion

The objective in the above dialogue was to avoid being pulled into a futile debate over the validity of Ricky's perceptions that no one could care about him and to shift the focus to how he would know if someone did. This is a subtle way of creating a broader range of possibilities than the narrow and rigid beliefs that Ricky presently holds. Although Ricky was not ready to embrace other interpretations of his interpersonal experience, these alternative views of reality were at least introduced in the dialogue.

Many children easily identify with *Blow-Up Bernie*. Impulsive-reactive aggression is common in children with anger control problems and is the result of a combination of neurobiological factors, temperamental predisposition, and the socio-cultural environment, interacting with many mediating influences. Impulsive-reactive aggression is different from the violence that results from the long-term and insidious effects of toxic social environments, environments that destroy the spirit and soul. Kenneth V. Hardy and Tracy Laszloffy (2005), in *Teens Who Hurt*, distinguish between anger and rage. Anger is defined as a reaction to a frustrating situation. Rage, on the other hand, has deep and long-term roots often resulting from invisible wounds to the soul, especially among those who grow up in socially toxic environments characterized by extreme poverty, exposure to domestic violence, high-crime neighborhoods, and violence in school. These detrimental influences eventually result in the loss of dignity, hope, faith in themselves, and reliance on others.

Child clinicians need to appreciate this distinction because anger management training is an inadequate response to children who suffer rage as a result of profound losses and crushing of their spirit. While anger management training is useful in helping children with tenuous impulse control and poor social skills, it doesn't address the complicated underlying emotional process related to invisible wounds resulting from repeated devaluation, humiliation, and degradation (Crenshaw & Hardy, 2005; Crenshaw & Hardy in press; Hardy & Crenshaw, in press).

In *The Lost Boys*, James Garbarino (1999) notes that he has never interviewed a youth facing charges for a violent crime that, upon closer examination, had not been traumatized. As in *Blow-Up Bernie*, these children view themselves as "bad kids" and the sense of "badness" is deeply entrenched in those who express rage resulting from underlying scars to their soul. Children prone to reactive-impulsive aggression also view themselves as "bad" because they are unable to stop, think, and reflect on their choices and, as a result, they frequently find themselves in trouble at home and at school. Their identity, however, is not crystallized around being a "bad kid" in the same way as those youth who suffer extreme devaluation, humiliation, and degradation. The loss of hope, dreams, and vision for a better life is one of the most painful and crushing of all the profound and repeated losses a child can experience.

When unaddressed trauma is at the core of a complicated underlying emotional process, a comprehensive treatment strategy is needed (Crenshaw and Garbarino, 2007; Crenshaw and Mordock, 2005a; Crenshaw and Mordock, 2005b; Crenshaw and Hardy, 2005; Crenshaw & Hardy, in press). Social skills training programs and anger management training can contribute to the child's ability to be successful within his or her social networks to include family, community, and culture. It should be noted that intensive individual treatment for youngsters with severe trauma is a rather rare event. Many—far too many—children are simply viewed as "bad kids" and as Hardy (2003) has noted, that is exactly what they receive: treatment (i.e., punishment) for "bad kids." While violence is an ugly and hideous poison in our world, and I denounce and deplore it as do Hardy (2003) and Garbarino (1999), imposing stiffer sentences on youth who already bear the scars of unrecognized and untreated trauma is not a viable solution to this vexing problem in our society.

Symbol Work with The Misunderstood Mouse

From a collection of miniatures, the child can select a symbol for the Misunderstood Mouse and also a symbol for each of the other mice that the child wishes to include. The child may want to introduce other characters as well as choose a symbol for each of them. The child can be invited to be the voice of the Misunderstood Mouse and the other mice or assign the therapist to be the voice of one or more of the characters. The follow-up of the choice of the symbols for each and the interplay between them can further enrich the therapeutic exchange.

Puppet Play with The Misunderstood Mouse

The child can also be invited to play out the story of *The Misunderstood Mouse* in puppet play. By introducing action either in puppet play or giving voice to the symbols as described above, it facilitates spontaneous expression similar to Oaklander's Gestalt approach (1988) and often takes the scenarios in directions where the child needs to go.

"MIKE'S VERSION OF RUSSIAN ROULETTE" (STRATEGY FOR CHILDREN AGES 12 TO 17)

Purpose: *Developing a strong self-observer, the capacity for self-awareness, reflection, the ability to plan, weigh the consequences, and make informed, reasoned decisions can literally be the difference between life and death during the teen years when high-risk behaviors tend to peak. Adolescents are known for emotional and impulsive decisions, poor judgments, and high-risk behavior that can include dangerous abuse of alcohol or substances, unsafe sexual behavior, and high speed and reckless driving. The dangerous behavior in some cases reflects underlying emotional* *distress, family conflict, or discouragement in academic pursuits, but perhaps more often is driven by the quest for peer acceptance. Sometimes these impulsive judgments result in disastrous consequences. The goal of this strategy is to initiate what can be difficult and sensitive discussions with teens about high-risk behaviors and to encourage reflection and cognitive inquiry to militate against impulsive and dangerous decisions. Adolescents are notoriously known for their "deafness" to parental cautions and warnings; "scare tactics" consisting of putting wrecks beside the highway to deter drinking and driving have been largely ineffective. But since this story is told within metaphor and even in the follow-up questions consistently remains in the metaphor, the hope is that teens will be able to reflect on some of the disastrous choices they can potentially make without feeling "preached" to and thereby be more likely to remember the story when they are faced with such similar high-risk temptations themselves.*

The Story (Due to the length of the story it is recommended that the story be given to the adolescent to read within a session)

"Mike was determined to be one of the 'cool kids.' He was quarterback on the high school football team, was an above average student although he could have done better if he put more time into his studies. He had a 'cool girlfriend' who was pretty and popular and lot of the other boys in his junior year class in Williams High School envied him. Mike had a lot going for him but somehow he still felt he had something to prove. Some of the really 'cool' guys in his high school were doing things such as playing 'chicken' or drag racing at high speeds with cars on isolated roads out of town that scared him. He also had stayed away from alcohol and drugs except for an occasional sip of beer at a party just to be social, but most of the time he would drink diet soda. At parties the majority of kids were drinking and some were smoking pot in back rooms of the house, almost always in the home of a student whose parents were out of town for the weekend. A few kids were experimenting with higher-risk drugs such as cocaine and ecstasy. It was not uncommon for some of his friends to get drunk and/or high on pot at one of these parties and slip into one of the back rooms to have sex with a girl. Most of these things Mike disapproved of and they made him uneasy. He was under pressure from his friends to join in because they were distressed by his obvious disapproval. Even his girlfriend, Sherry, suggested that he should 'loosen up' a little.

"One night Mike was hanging out with some guys down by the dock on a lake, when Eric drove up and parked next to where they were standing. Eric was nineteen and was known in the community as a tough guy and a risk-taker. For reasons unknown, he never liked Mike. Eric was out of school and worked in a garage so Mike was relieved that he no longer saw him that often. Eric opened the passenger car door and stared at Mike and said, 'Come on yellow-belly let's go for a ride.' Mike just stared back. Eric began to taunt him. 'What's the matter candy-ass? Don't tell me you are afraid to get into the car with me?' The other boys were snickering. Mike was scared and his better judgment was that it would be stupid to get into the car. Eric had obviously been drinking and he was known for his high-speed and reckless driving. Eric continued, 'I've always known you were a chicken.' This was a direct assault on Mike's manhood and impulsively, he started toward the car. His good friend Rob tried to stop him. Rob said, 'Mike you are crazy, don't do it.' But Mike pushed Rob out of the way, jumped in the passenger seat, and slammed the door. Eric peeled out and took off down the highway. The guys standing at the dock laughed nervously, except for Rob and a couple of Mike's other good friends who just stood there silently in shock.

"Almost immediately, Mike knew he had made a terrible mistake in judgment. Eric was laughing and obviously enjoying the fact that he had Mike in a place where he could torture him by taking him 'on the ride of his life.' Before long, as Eric reached speeds exceeding ninety miles an hour, Mike prayed that this would not be a ride that ended his life. He was in total panic mode as his life flashed past him in his mind. He realized he might not ever see Sherry again or Rob or any of his other good friends, his parents, and his sister, his golden retriever Max, who had been his companion since early childhood. He was willing to put his life on the line just to prove his 'manliness.' It was too late to correct his impulsive decision. To jump out of the car would mean certain death and to stay in the car looked like a death sentence as well. He kept thinking, 'I am too young to die. I am only seventeen.'"

"He decided to plead with Eric and admit his fear. He decided he would rather be viewed as a coward than a brave dead but foolish kid. He shouted, 'Slow down, please, you are scaring me!' Eric laughed and speeded up more. Mike said, 'Please, I don't want to die.' Eric laughed even harder. A few moments later, Eric began to slow down, Mike sighed with relief. He thought his ordeal was about to end. To his absolute horror, however, Eric turned on to a back road and told Mike, 'Now you are going to see what it is like to really die.'"

"The back road was narrow, with steep hills, and curves. Mike was thinking, 'This guy is either really drunk or totally out of his mind; I am going to die in a car with a madman and I was the one who decided to get into the car with him.' Mike closed his eyes because he couldn't bear to watch as Eric drove at insane speed on a road that was not built for high speeds. Once Eric opened his eyes just long enough to see that they were approaching the crest of a hill and the speedometer read eighty-five miles an hour. Eric, in his drunken state, didn't even bother to stay to the right on this narrow road.

Mike knew if a car was coming the other way it would mean certain death for everyone in the two cars.

"Mike never opened his eyes again until the car stopped. He was white as a sheet and he felt sick at his stomach. When he opened the door and realized he was back at the dock he could barely stand up. Eric was still laughing when he got out of the car and shouted, 'I hope you enjoyed the ride,' as Mike slammed the door. Eric then sped off. Mike looked around but there was no one there. The guys who he had intended to impress didn't even bother to hang around to see if he survived the consequences of his impulsive, reckless decision. Never in his whole life had he felt so foolish but he also felt grateful just to be alive. When he reached his car, Rob was sitting in the passenger seat. He drove Rob home, neither boy said a word. They didn't have to."

Drawing Directives (Optional Step)

"Now try to get a picture in your mind of Mike either before he gets in the car with Eric or while on this terrifying ride and draw it as best you can. If you prefer you can draw a picture of the look on Mike's face when he thought for sure he was going to die."

Note to Clinicians: In order to increase the chance that this story will be effective in leaving a vivid memory in the pre-teen's or adolescent's mind of how potentially catastrophic an impulsive, reckless decision can be, and conversely to facilitate the capacity for reflection and careful decision making, it has been suggested in the lead-in to this strategy that clinicians remain in the metaphor throughout. This is because teens tend to tune out when they feel adults, and especially parents are either "lecturing," or "moralizing," or "preaching" to them. Of course, if pre-teens or adolescents step out of the metaphor to discuss directly how this issue pertains to them, it would be important to honor their wish to relate this to their own life.

Follow-Up to the Drawing

1. Tell me about your drawing.
2. What title do you choose for your drawing?
3. What do you think Mike learned from his night of horror?
4. Why do you think that Mike and Rob didn't say anything on the drive home?
5. What advice do you think Rob would give Mike if he were to face a situation like this again?

6. Mike went against his better judgment when he got into the car with Eric. What factors made it hard for him to say no in this situation?
7. What do you make of the fact that the kid who waited for Mike to return was Rob (the one person who tried to stop him from getting in the car)?
8. Why do you think the other kids who were bystanders didn't bother to stay around?

Storytelling Directives

"Now I would like you to imagine how this experience affected or changed Mike's life. Create a story about Mike after his death-tempting experience. Include in your story any changes in Mike's relationships with his friends, Sherry, his girlfriend, Rob, and his other friends. Also, include in your story any changes he made in handling similar situations that might arise in the future."

Follow-Up to the Story

1. What title would you give to your story?
2. Who was most affected by Mike's night of terror in your story?
3. What was the biggest change noticed in Mike after his near-death experience?
4. Supposed Mike was invited to speak to a group of middle school students about the risks of accepting a dare, what do you think would be the main points he would make?
5. How do you think Mike's life will turn out in the long run?
6. How do you think Eric's life will turn out in the long run?
7. Do you think that Mike would ever tell his parents about this experience?
8. Do you think he would ever tell his girlfriend about this experience?
9. Do you think that he and Rob eventually talked about what happened?
10. Do you think any changes that Mike made were long-lasting?
11. Do you think the kids at the dock respected Mike more or less after he got in the car with Eric? Explain why.
12. Do you think that if Mike told Sherry, his girlfriend, what happened that she would respect him more or less after his decision? Explain why.

Symbol Work with this Strategy

Instead of drawing the images stimulated by the story or in addition, the therapist can ask the teen to pick a symbol from an assortment of miniatures to represent the main characters: Mike, Eric, and Rob and perhaps the other guys who were bystanders in the story. On inquiry, the therapist can explore why a given symbol was chosen for each person. Alternatively, the adolescent could be asked to pick a symbol to represent Mike's feelings at different points in the story such as when he went to a party, when he was at the dock with the other guys, when Eric pulled up and taunted him to get in the car, when Rob tried to stop him from getting in the car, when he got into the car, during the worse parts of the ride, when he got out of the car, and finally, when he drove home with Rob. The therapist can then explore the choice of symbols in each instance.

Discussion

Bessel van der Kolk (2003) explained that with traumatized children—and I would add with impulsive kids as well—our job as clinicians is partly to build and strengthen the frontal lobe of the brain. The frontal lobe of the brain is the seat of executive functioning, the ability to plan, organize, remember, reflect, consider consequences, and to make decisions accordingly. Neuroscience research has shown that the brain during adolescence undergoes some major reorganization that leaves adolescents somewhat vulnerable to impulsive actions and choices. The neuro-pathways between the cortical frontal areas of the brain and the limbic system are not as highly developed as they are later in young adulthood.

While the brain is developing the neuro-connecting fibers during adolescence the adolescent is less capable of exercising in an optimal way the cortical control and modulation of the more emotional centers of the brain and this can be a recipe for the kind of risk that Mike exposes himself to in the story. This strategy like the others in this book designed for teens are intended to engage adolescents in difficult therapeutic conversations that they tend to avoid due to the sensitive nature of the topic and the emotional charge and often guilt or shame associated with these issues.

Teens in a desperate attempt to gain peer approval engage in high-risk behavior that sometimes results in unthinkable tragedy. All too often, I have been called to consult in high schools after tragic accidents, often associated with alcohol, which has resulted in the death of one or more young teen boys and/or girls. Those experiences affected me deeply as I tried to help their friends, teachers, and families cope with such an unbearable loss, one that in many cases could have been prevented with some reflection and better judgment.

Nationally in a survey, slightly over 40 percent of students had used marijuana one or more times during their lifetimes and 10 percent had used marijuana for the first time before age 13 (O'Sullivan, 2005). Nearly 9 percent of students had used a form of cocaine; 12 percent had sniffed glue, breathed the contents of aerosol spray cans, or inhaled paints or sprays to get high; close to 8 percent of students had used methampthetamines one or more times in their life; over 11 percent had used ecstasy one or more times; and over 3 percent had used heroin one or more times (O'Sullivan, 2005). Adolescents also sometimes use powerful and potentially dangerous prescription pain prescriptions such as Oxycontin to self-medicate not physical but emotional pain.

A study looking at risky driving and its correlated lifestyle features found that boys who displayed risky driving habits were more likely to be engaged in a lifestyle that was characterized by high involvement with antisocial behaviors, tobacco smoking, comfort eating and time spent in non-organized activities with friends (Bina, Graziano, and Bonino, 2006). These researchers also report that girls involved in risky driving were more likely to also be engaged in other risk-taking behaviors, antisocial behaviors, and drug use.

In an analysis of risk and adolescent decision making, Reyna and Farley (2006) observe that adolescent goals tend to lean toward maximizing immediate pleasure. They explain that in a moment of high excitement, passion, or with the encouragement of peers, adolescents are likely to reason more poorly than adults do. Reyna and Farley also note that brain maturation in adolescence is incomplete and that impulsivity, thrill seeking, and depression contribute to the risk of poor decision making. They describe a dual process model in approaches to risk taking: a reasoned and a reactive route. The storytelling strategy of *Mike's Version of Russian Roulette* is intended to strengthen the "reasoned" route and to curb the "reactive" path, which all too often adolescents are prone to, sadly at times with tragic consequences.

A very interesting study reports that families can assist in developing the all-important skills of reflection as well as reinforce family bonds and values by increasing family dinner meal frequency (Fulkerson, Story, Mellin, Leffert, Newmark-Sztainer, and French, 2006). These investigators found that frequency of family meals is an external developmental asset or protective factor that tended to decrease the risk of all high-risk behaviors measured which included substance use, sexual activity, depression/suicide, antisocial behaviors, violence, school problems, binge eating/purging, and excessive weight loss. It is amazing to realize how this ritual of family togetherness and sharing can exert such a powerful positive influence on adolescent development.

How These Strategies Can Enhance the Therapeutic Process

All of the strategies in this chapter are designed to support children and teens through their identification with the characters in the stories to strengthen their capacity for deeper self-observation. The story of the *Wise Ole Owl* is written specifically to examine a deeper purpose and meaning to life to the extent that developmental constraints allow. The other three stories, *Blow-Up Bernie, The Misunderstood Mouse,* and *Mike's Version of Russian Roulette,* are designed to further the capacity for children and in the case of Mike, adolescents, to examine motives, choices, and consequences when acting. Children in clinical settings, particularly impulsive, highly emotionally reactive children tend to operate on "high-octane" momentum. They are prone to reap the predictable and often unfortunate consequences of poor planning, ill-considered decisions, emotionally labile responses that impair their relationships with others and often damage their self-esteem. It is difficult to feel good about yourself if you are always in trouble or you habitually alienate others.

Because these children do not pause and reflect, they are not good at making transitions and they simply barrel down the track like a runaway locomotive. When they "crash and burn" they have little insight or understanding as to how they got into such a jam. What these children lack are the meta-awareness skills, the "executive functioning" skills, mediated in the prefrontal cortex of the brain. Siegel (2007) explained, "The middle prefrontal regions are an important contributor to self-observation and metacognition: We can have an image of ourselves in the past, present, and future and we also map out the nature of our own mind's activities. It is here where we see the potential neural contribution to the idea that mindful awareness is more than simply being aware: In mindfulness, we actively perceive our own mind and are aware of our awareness" (p. 110).

The mindfulness that Siegel (2007) described is essential in order for children as well as adults to be "captains of their own ships" and to make fully conscious and responsible choices that will not lead to sorrow. Since the skills of self-observation are practiced within the metaphors of the stories and the identifications with story characters, it lays the groundwork for more in-depth reflection and examination than would be possible if these issues were approached directly.

· 6 ·

Facilitating Empathy for Self and Others

Overview: *To be able to appreciate, understand, and respond with warmth and empathy for the pain of another is one of the most pivotal of all capacities allowing for close and satisfying connections with other human beings. Empathy is easier to define than to implement. Even young children show the emerging capacity for empathy when a toddler comforts another child who falls down and scrapes a knee on the playground. It is hard, however, for humans, particularly when in conflict with others, to appreciate the other's point of view and feelings. Empathy requires careful listening. It is an exceedingly difficult human feat to suspend one's own point of view and emotional responses in order to intensely concentrate on understanding the point of view and emotions of another. The strategies in this chapter focus on developing and strengthening the capacity for empathy.*

"THE NEW ALLIGATOR IN THE SWAMP"
(AGES 5 TO 8)

Purpose: *The spontaneous symbolic play of children offers the child therapist numerous opportunities through the metaphor of the play characters to teach, model, and practice empathy for self and others. Most children will be able to identify with the alligator in this play scenario because nearly every child will have had some experience with being the "new kid on the block" with all the anxiety that attends to being the newcomer. Children are redundant in the play themes that are emotionally powerful for them. Sometimes that is useful to both child and therapist because the child has numerous opportunities for gradual exposure and attempts at mastery and it may benefit the therapist because the redundancy gives more opportunity for the therapist to identify central themes. Children get stuck, however, at times and*

83

the repetitions serve no purpose except to increase the frustration and helplessness of the child. When this is happening, it is important that the therapist intervene to free the child by introducing new variations and possibilities.

Directive Symbolic Play Interventions

It is important to introduce greater variation and complexity when young children are playing out repetitive themes of helplessness. If, for example, they repetitiously take play animals or puppets and line up all the powerful, menacing creatures on one side (often their side) and all the weak, vulnerable creatures on the other side (often the therapist's side) they are getting stuck in a process that is not helpful and, in fact, may be harmful because it reinforces their sense of powerlessness that is displaced, in this instance on the therapist. The therapist can begin to nudge them into altering the drama. The therapist can enlist strong and wise allies on the vulnerable side to fend off the powerful monsters and aggressors or use invisible shields or secret weapons to keep the aggressors at bay.

Themes of fun can be introduced since no army is at battle all the time. The idea of inviting a peacemaker, like Jimmy Carter, can be introduced to meet with them, to give them some tips on how to negotiate and settle their differences. This represents a considerable expansion of the endless re-enactment of the "kill or be killed" theme and suggests other possibilities for constructive and effective action and more importantly can lead to greater empathy and understanding between both sides of the conflict.

Clinical Illustration: Charlie (age 6)

Charlie's spontaneous symbolic play early in therapy began with the turtle puppet afraid to come out of his shell. The therapist coaxed the turtle out of his shell. Then the alligator puppet begins attacking all the other puppets. The therapist directs the other animals to cautiously approach the alligator and explain that this is a friendly swamp. "The alligator doesn't have to hurt others because this is a safe and friendly place where no one will hurt him." However, as Charlie takes the role of the other animal puppets, they attack the alligator and there are big fights with injuries on both sides.

The animals were sent one at a time but couldn't resist attacking the alligator (the bumblebee stung the alligator) because they did not trust the alligator would not hurt them. I repeatedly made reflections such as, "Oh, the animals don't understand that the alligator won't hurt them once he realizes that he is in a safe place and no one is going to hurt him." When the animals continued attacking the alligator, the therapist continued with reflections,

"Oh, they don't trust that the alligator won't hurt them so they would rather bite than take a chance of being bitten. So they are scared too. It is sad that everyone is afraid but instead of realizing that is the problem, they try to hurt each other and nothing changes." Finally, Charlie realized that he could not enact the friendly approach that the therapist was coaching him to do, so he gave the therapist another alligator puppet and asked if the other alligator (therapist) would talk to the alligator?

The alligator (therapist) said, "Oh there is now another alligator in the swamp. Oh, I am so glad now I can have another alligator as a friend. Welcome to the swamp, Mr. Alligator, you will find out that most of the animals here are friendly once you get to know them and they get to know you. You will be able to make friends with most of them. Once in a while somebody will get in a bad mood and do something mean but they are mostly friendly animals, and they won't hurt you. I remember when I first came to the swamp I was scared and I didn't understand that the animals are friendly here. I started going after everybody in a mean way. I wanted to let them know that they were not going to hurt me. It took me a long time to realize that they did not want to hurt me, yet I was hurting them. I hope you don't make the same mistakes that I did because I made them afraid of me and it took a long time before they felt safe around me."

At that point "a switch moment" (Sarnoff, 1987) occurred as Charlie abruptly ended this play scenario and took out the doctor's kit and began administering to the wounds of the various animals. He checked their blood pressure, heart rate, and temperature. The therapist responded to their physical pains as metaphors of emotional pain, so if their blood pressure was high, the therapist reflected, "Oh, he must be upset, I wonder if he is still scared or angry? Doctor, what do you think would have upset the turtle that much? Charlie would quickly correct the therapist and say, "Oh, he is not upset, he is just hurt—his leg was hurt from a bite wound. He and the alligator had a fight." The therapist pushed it a little further and said, "Maybe he is upset about that." Then Charlie brought in the alligator and he had injuries too. The therapist reflected, "It is not easy to come to the swamp and not know if the other animals are going to be friendly or mean. He must have been scared and upset." The therapist emphasized how kind and gentle the doctor (Charlie) was with the animals and what wonderful care he was taking of the wounded animals.

Discussion

Charlie gave me a running head start in deciding how to intervene with his play by spontaneously seeking out the turtle puppet that did not want to come out of his shell. Although Charlie had been aggressive to other kids at school and did not have many friends, like so many kids his anger masked his fear. In the subsequent play he shifted identifications between the aggressor alligator who also was hiding his fear and the other animal puppets who were afraid also, but disguised by aggressive attacks on the alligator. Likewise, Charlie was new to therapy and like the turtle he sought out initially, he was not sure if it was safe to come out of his shell.

Like the alligator that had to be convinced that the swamp was a safe and friendly place and the other animals who had to be assured that the newcomer to the swamp would not hurt them, Charlie was not sure if therapy was going to be a safe place and whether the newcomer to his life was a trustworthy person. After I reflected the underlying fear of both the alligator who was new to the swamp and the animals who were fearful of approaching this new creature, he shifted to healing play in which he attended tenderly to the wounds of the animals as well as the alligator. This shift told me that Charlie "got it." He understood that he was not going to be hurt in this "new place," and that he could at least entertain the idea of healing in the same way that he gently attended to the injuries of the animals.

Therapeutic play has two characteristics that continue to amaze me after nearly four decades of clinical work with children. One is the ability of young children to condense into rich metaphors, often in the first session, the core of their hurt or in some cases trauma, and communicate it symbolically through their play. If we look and listen closely, we will "see" and "hear" their symbolic communication. The other striking feature of symbolic play is its healing power for young children (Gil, 1991). When they are finished working through their life dramas, they are ready to move on and the therapeutic play loses his compelling attraction and value for them.

"THE ANIMAL THAT NO ONE WANTS TO HUG" (STRATEGY FOR AGES 7 TO 12)

I am grateful to Dr. Joyce C. Mills whose presentation on June 5th, 2004, to the New York Association of Play Therapy in Buffalo, New York, was entitled, "How to Hug a Porcupine." Her use of this clever metaphor inspired me to write this story.

Purpose: *This story explores the child's capacity for empathy. Many children will identify with the plight of the porcupine, especially aggressive children who have a way of "sticking their quills" into anyone who comes too close. Yet, as the story unfolds it becomes clear that all that self-protection comes at a steep price, namely,* *social isolation and loneliness. Research has shown that aggressive children are not only more at risk than other kids for externalizing disorders but internalizing disorders as well including depression. Those children who closely identify with the porcupine will tell stories when they take the voice of the porcupine that will be of interest to the therapist, not only in terms of their capacity for empathy but also for self-awareness.*

The Story

"One group of animals exists that if you get too close to them, you are almost certain to be hurt. Do you know what animals I am talking about? There are many large animals in the wild that might hurt you if you invaded their territory or came too close to them, such as, tigers and lions. But I am thinking of an animal that is often encountered on hikes that a group of friends took in the Catskill Mountains in upstate New York. One of the friends, Lewis, had a beautiful Golden Retriever named Teddy. Teddy was a wonderful dog and everyone loved him. But one day Teddy made the mistake of getting too close to this animal and poor Teddy was in awful pain because his face was covered with sharp quills. Now you know that I am talking about porcupines. Lewis had to pull each quill out of Teddy's face one at a time, causing Teddy still more pain.

"The three men often encountered porcupines on their hikes but the porcupines never once acted aggressive or, in anyway, threatened them. Nevertheless, Teddy thought this was a playful animal and gave it a playful nudge. But think about the story from the porcupine's point of view.

"The porcupine is better equipped than just about any creature of its size to defend itself against natural enemies. So when Lewis and his friends, Dave and Gary, encountered a porcupine on the trail, it didn't need to be aggressive because its coat of quills was all the defense and offense that a small animal could desire. This kind of protection, however, may come at a high price. Let's be curious about the story of a porcupine. It would seem that not one animal, not even its mother or father, could give the porcupine a hug or snuggle up to it. Perhaps the porcupine wishes that, at least sometimes, it could shed its coat of quills and be able to romp and play with friendly animals.

"It would be hard to find a more lovable, friendlier animal than Teddy and he was out having a fun romp in the woods. He had no intentions of hurting the porcupine, but never having tangled with one before, he thought it would be great fun to give it a playful nudge. How sadly mistaken poor Teddy was. The porcupine's natural shield of sharp quills does not distinguish between playful friend and dangerous enemy. So the porcupine missed out on this special opportunity for play and fun with this wonderful golden retriever that everyone loved—how sad for Teddy, but also how sad for the porcupine."

Drawing Directives

"Try to picture that porcupine in your mind. You may close your eyes if you wish, use your imagination to get a clear picture of what the porcupine looks like. When you are ready, if your eyes are closed, gently open them and draw the porcupine as best as you can."

Some Considerations for the Therapist

1. Is the porcupine drawn alone or with Teddy or other animals?
2. Are there any people included in the picture? (Some children, especially those uncomfortable in the human world, often fantasize about being alone with animals or in a sanctuary in the natural world. Since people were in the story their omission in the child's drawing may be of significance.)
3. Is there action in the picture (e.g., a chase, a fight)? What is the nature of the action? Aggression? Flight?

Follow-Up Questions

1. What title would you like to give to the picture?
2. Pretend that the porcupine and any other animals included in the picture, such as Teddy, could talk. What would they say?
3. What is the porcupine feeling in your picture?
4. What is Teddy feeling?
5. Do you think Teddy will want to go on other hikes after his experience with the porcupine?
6. If you were an animal which would you prefer to be: Teddy or the porcupine? Explain why.
7. Do you think there is anyway to hug a porcupine?
8. Do you think the porcupine would like a hug? Why?

Storytelling Directives

"Now, I want you to try hard to imagine what the life story of a porcupine might be. Let's pretend that you have been chosen to be the voice of the porcupine and to tell his story to the other animals. Perhaps the other animals, like Teddy, have learned the hard way to stay away from porcupines, but never stopped to consider what life is like for a porcupine. Imagine being a porcupine, well-protected, shielded with sharp quills all over your body. No one dares to come too close to you, not even the friendliest of animals, like Teddy. Once an animal like Teddy gets a face full of quills, it is almost certain that the animal will never come close to you again. Try to put yourself inside the skin of the porcupine. Are you lonely? Are you sad? Are you angry? Do you like it the way it is? You are well-protected but cut off from everyone? Would there be any changes you would want to make? Be the voice of the porcupine and tell its story so the other animals can understand and really feel what it is like to be a porcupine.

"So all the animals in the Catskill Mountains sent a representative to the top of Blackhead Mountain on the night when the porcupine agreed to tell its story. Teddy was there, and so was the black bear, the mountain lion, the squirrel, the snake, and so on, and they all were eager to hear the story of the porcupine. The porcupine began, 'My fellow animals, my friends, and my enemies in the Catskill Mountains, I wish to thank you for giving me this chance to tell my life story. I am going to start from the beginning, but my story has a middle part and an ending. It all began when I was born right over there on Thomas Cole Mountain. I was . . .'" (Child continues from here.)

Follow-Up to the Story

1. What title would you chose for your story?
2. What can be learned from your story?
3. Were the animals of the Catskills surprised by the story of the porcupine?
4. Do you think the animals will be more patient and understanding of the porcupine after hearing its story?
5. Do you think the porcupine will feel less lonely after telling his story to the other animals?
6. Do you think Teddy will feel differently toward the porcupine after listening to his story?
7. Do you think any of the animals would stick up for the porcupine after hearing its story? If so, which one?
8. Do you think any of the animals would want to trade places with the porcupine?

For Children Who No Longer Need the Symbolic Shelter of the Metaphor

9. Who in your family is more like Teddy?
10. Who in your family is more like the porcupine?

Discussion

The dilemma of the porcupine reflects the struggle of many resistant children brought to therapy. They have developed a good offense and, like the porcupine, a good defense as well. They do not allow others to get too close. It is difficult to get to know them and to learn their life stories. By taking the voice of the porcupine, they may, to a degree, be able to express, through the metaphor (from a safe symbolic distance), the story of what it is like to be isolated and cut off from others and how being in that situation feels. It gives them an opportunity to practice the crucial skill of empathy, to take the place of the porcupine and to imagine what it must feel like.

This strategy can also lead to greater self-empathy and understanding. If children can appreciate the dilemma and pain of the porcupine, they may come to see themselves in a new light and not just "a bad kid." Some children can explore the meaning of their story directly, since the porcupine's anguish goes right to the heart of the resistant child's painful struggles. For others, it can be more productive to remain within the safety of the metaphor. One way to accomplish this task is to set up a question and answer session after the porcupine speaks. The child can remain as the voice of the porcupine and the therapist assumes the voice of all the other animals. Some sample questions follow:

1. "My name is Teddy and you probably don't remember me, but I sure remember you. Did you mean to hurt me as badly as you did? I only wanted to play with you. I never wanted to hurt you."
2. The bear asks, "Did you always have that coat of sharp quills?"
3. The mountain lion asks, "Do you ever wish that you could take that coat off? Even if it's just for a short time?"
4. The deer asks, "How do you think your life would have been different if you didn't always have your coat of quills on?"
5. The rabbit asks, "If you had a kind heart, how would anyone know?"
6. The fox pipes up and asks, "If you could be a different animal what animal would you choose to be?"
7. The snake follows by asking, "Why did you pick that animal?"
8. The chipmunk said, "I am just a little guy myself, I am wondering has anyone ever hurt you badly?"
9. The coyote had a final question, "Has anyone ever helped you? If so, how?"

Mark's Drawing (age 12)   "This man fell and landed on the porcupine, he ended up getting a mouthful and handful of quills. It was a bad day for both."

Drawing 6.1.   "The Animal That Nobody Wants to Hug"

This brief explanation of Drawing 6.1 is interesting because Mark, although doing much better at the time of this drawing, had a history of emotional and impulse regulation problems and frequently was out-of-sync with his surrounding world. It would be easy for Mark to identify with this unfortunate man who tripped at just the wrong time and landed on of all things, a porcupine! Mark has had plenty of experience of being in the wrong place at the wrong time, doing something that was inappropriate at the time, and finding himself facing unpleasant and unanticipated consequences.

This strategy enabled Mark to talk about the kind of anguish he feels by having "too much offense" ("You can't fire me, I quit") and thereby ending up like the porcupine lonely and isolated. His strong identification with the porcupine was revealed in the follow-up to his drawing that led him to go further than previously in sharing these feelings. When he talked with his family about the drawing and his consistent feelings of "always being in the wrong place at the wrong time" and ending up ostracized like the porcupine, it enabled his family to have a much greater appreciation of what Mark was feeling inside. Consequently, they were able to be more compassionate and supportive toward him.

Mark's story is very typical of the experience of ADHD children and other youth with disruptive behavior disorders who frequently find themselves in trouble as a result of poor judgment, bad timing, and facing unanticipated and unpleasant consequences. The impaired social judgment and lack of social awareness in addition to weak visual spatial skills and motor skills are also frequently seen in children with Non-Verbal Learning Disabilities (Rourke, 1995).

These children are often mistaken for ADHD children in the early school grades because their poor visual-spatial skills frequently make them look like they are not able to focus when instead they receive so little information from their visual processing that they simply don't bother looking at people; they make very poor eye contact. Often these children are tuned in, however, through their usually good auditory processing skills. Their weak motor skills, however, may lead them to frequently bump into others, thus once again making it more likely that they will be mistakenly viewed as ADHD.

Whatever the cause of the child's social ineptness or ostracism, the story that most children tell about the porcupine's loneliness and isolation resonates with many of them. The question that invariably chokes me up is when I take the voice of the rabbit, and ask the porcupine, "If you had a kind heart, how would anyone know?" I find this captures the heartbreaking experience of so many children. No one is able to get close enough to know if inside that child, shielded by all manner of protection, resides a kind and tender heart.

Directed Symbolic Play with Puppets

This story is easily given more dramatic impact by having the child choose the dog or porcupine puppet and acting it out. Children find the porcupine puppet one of the most intriguing puppets in my office. In most cases they are likely to choose the porcupine but sometimes they identify with Teddy because of all the "quills that have hurt them." Another choice would be to move into puppet play at the point of questions after the child takes the voice of the porcupine and tells its story. This is likely to result in more affective impact.

In many cases, the children will identify with both puppets and may choose to move back and forth and assume the voices of both the porcupine and Teddy or perhaps the other animal puppets as well. Children usually have experience with being in both the aggressor and victimized role and like the porcupine, have more than enough experience with being misunderstood. Like the porcupine, they also overinterpret signs of danger and are adept at keeping others at a distance.

Therapeutic Use of Symbols

The child in an individual, group, or family session could be asked to pick a symbol (miniature) to represent the porcupine, Teddy, the other animals, as well as the feelings of the porcupine and Teddy at the time of the encounter between them. The child could be asked to pick another symbol to represent Teddy's feelings toward the porcupine after the porcupine has told its story. This may be a good indication of the child's capacity for empathy if the symbols signify a shift in Teddy's view of the porcupine after listening to the porcupine's story.

Discussion

This story elicits the capacity for the most important of all pro-social skills—the ability to empathize with others. In this case, the empathy is not only for the porcupine, but also for the child who closely identifies with the plight of the porcupine. Self-empathy is usually required before genuine empathy for others can develop.

Self-empathy can be fostered by the therapist's acceptance of the child. The child will gradually internalize the warmth, compassion, and caring expressed by the therapist and such internalization may be one of the chief gains made by a wounded child in intensive therapy. This in turn lays the groundwork for development of the capacity of empathy, a crucial factor in breaking the cycle of aggression and later the potential for violence (Fraiberg, Adelson, and Shapiro, 1965; Garbarino, 1999; Crenshaw and Mordock, 2005a, 2005b; Crenshaw and Hardy, 2005; Hardy and Laszloffy, 2005; Crenshaw and Garbarino, 2007). Like the porcupine, the children may have experienced little closeness with and acceptance by others. Each child's story may yield important clues as to where they are in the development of the capacity for empathy.

Empathy involves multiple skills, including the ability to take the perspective of another and to appreciate this perspective on both a cognitive and affective level (Epley, Savitsky, and Gilovich, 2002). The latter capacity is especially underdeveloped in aggressive children. Some children can display skill at perspective taking and cognitive understanding of another's position, but they display no affect when doing so—no true empathy.

It is through the healing experience of acceptance by the therapist that the child learns to internalize the empathy, compassion, and genuine warmth of the therapist and begins to develop the capacities for self-acceptance, self-empathy, and self-compassion. The unwavering commitment of a caring adult conveys a message that is a powerful vote of confidence and faith in the child that can be uplifting to even the most despairing and demoralized child. These children expect adults to give up on them and act out in accordance with that belief. When the adult stays the course it can provide a corrective emotional experience and greatly aid in repairing the shame-based, stigmatized, painful sense of self.

Research on Empathy   Research studies have shown that children and adolescents with externalizing problems show a diminished capacity for empathy and caring behaviors. In studies by Zahn-Waxler and her colleagues (Zahn-Waxler, Usher, Suomi, and Cole, 2005; Hastings, Zahn-Waxler, Robinson, Usher, and Bridges, 2000) they found that by six or seven years old, the children identified in preschool to have clinical levels of externalizing problems exhibited decreased observed concern for others. In addition, research has shown that positive parenting (warmth, modeling prosocial behavior, using clear, firm explanations about the feelings of distress of others when hurt) facilitates the concern of children for others over time whereas negative parenting (family climate with low cohesion, marital dissatisfaction, and conflict) diminished the capacity of children for empathy over time (Zahn-Waxler, Park, Essex, Slattery, and Cole, 2005).

A study in Spain of empathy in children ten to twelve years old found that participants with high empathy showed many positive social behaviors (prosocial, assertive, consideration for others, self-control, leadership); few negative social behaviors (passive, aggressive, antisocial, withdrawal) and many assertive strategies of social interaction; that they were named as prosocial classmates; and that they had high self-concept (Garaigordobil and de Galdeano, 2006). It is interesting that the investigators found significant gender differences with girls exhibiting higher levels of empathy than boys.

Results in a study of gender effects on empathy in a group of adolescent African Americans indicated that youth with more empathy reported more prosocial behavior, and this effect was more pronounced for males than females (McMahon, Wernsman, and Parnes, 2006). These researchers explained that the findings suggest that the ability to understand another's perspective may be important in the development and expression of prosocial behaviors, particularly among males.

The "Safe Place" Is Created Only in an Empathic Context   Children will not share their stories, even through the symbolic haven and distance of play unless they are convinced that an empathic healer is present. If the child does not have a trusting relationship with an adult perceived to be caring and capable of responding to their pain in an empathic way they will not feel safe and nothing therapeutic will happen. This process cannot be rushed, pressured, or forced. It has to evolve in a natural way as a result of the child or family gradually coming to view the healer as committed to their well-being and competent and caring enough to see them through the arduous journey of facing and learning to live with the worst moments and sometimes horror if not trauma of their early lives.

"EMPATHY FOR OTHERS AND SELF" THE HEARTFELT FEELINGS COLORING CARD STRATEGIES (HFCCS) (RELATIONAL SERIES)

Purpose: In this variation of the HFCCS, the goal is to facilitate greater empathy for others and self. It is hard to overemphasize the role of empathy in the healthy social development of children. A vast child development literature has shown that positive social functioning in childhood is the most robust predictor of successful adjustment to adult life. A key feature of prosocial functioning is the ability to identify with and empathize with the feelings of others. These two skills seem to be intertwined so that if we are unable to identify with someone we are unlikely to empathize with that person and vice versa.

Step 1: Directions to the Child

"I want you to think about a child you know who made poor choices that led to trouble. Maybe it was something they did wrong at school, at home, or even in the community. Perhaps this child got in trouble with the police. Many kids get into trouble of some kind during the process of growing up so I am sure you can think of someone, probably more than one, who was in this situation at one time or another. When you have picked someone, please draw that person inside the heart on the front of the card or if you prefer you can draw your own heart and the person inside."

Step 2: Follow-Up

1. Tell me why you picked this person.
2. What kind of trouble did this person get into?
3. How did you feel when you first heard about this?
4. How well do you know this person?
5. How do you feel about this person?
6. How did you feel about the punishment that this person received?
7. What do you think this person felt when in trouble?

Step 3: Directions to the Child

"Please write a note to the person on the right inside panel of the card expressing your feelings about what happened to this person. Try to put yourself in this child's place and imagine what that must have felt like for that person to be in trouble at school, at home, or in the community."

Step 4: Follow-Up

1. What are some reasons that kids get into trouble?
2. Do you think kids sometimes act without thinking and when they get into trouble they are just as surprised as everyone else?
3. What do you think are some of the reasons that some kids get into trouble often?
4. Do you know someone who gets into trouble often?
5. Do you think the adults understand why such a boy or girl is often in trouble?
6. Do you understand why this happened with this particular child?
7. Have you ever tried to help a friend in trouble? If so can you tell about that experience?
8. What advice would you give to adults trying to help kids in trouble?

Discussion

It is not just the adults who sometimes view kids in trouble in a narrow way as simply "bad kids" but children buy into these negative labels as well and don't always see a basis for identifying and empathizing with another child in trouble. Thus, children may be harsh in their judgments of others as well as themselves when it is their turn to be in trouble for one reason or another. This is not to argue that guilt is not appropriate when a person commits wrongful acts toward another. The research of Tangney and Dearing (2002) convincingly demonstrates that guilt as defined by condemnation of a specific act of wrongdoing is a prosocial, constructive emotion and children with a capacity for feeling appropriate guilt tend in longitudinal studies to be better adjusted socially than those that lack such capacity.

Rather, it is shame that we wish to dispute and challenge. Tangney and Dearing (2002) define shame in contrast to guilt, as condemnation of self. If a child views others or self as "bad" or "evil" or "no good" then they have crossed the line into shame territory, which is associated with a wide range of psychopathology and poor outcomes in the Tangney and Dearing longitudinal research.

How These Strategies Can Enhance the Therapy Process

An important goal of therapy is to provide an emotionally corrective experience through a healing relationship that promotes trust and enhances the sense of worthiness and value of self. If an adult can find something redeeming and of value in children, they will begin to gradually believe in their worthiness. Likewise, if the child can see something redeeming in the porcupine and the child chronically in trouble, chances are good that the child will also be able to see something worthwhile within self.

When children can, to any extent, put themselves in the place of the porcupine and the child who is repeatedly in trouble and appreciate the feelings of each, it is an encouraging and hopeful prognostic sign. In the case of Mark, it opened up feelings through his identification with the ostracized porcupine that he had not been able to talk about previously since his impulsive behavior had built a barrier between him and his peers that was just as isolating as the sharp quills of the porcupine.

Many aggressive children are totally stymied by the task of showing empathy, at least at the beginning of the therapeutic process. The importance of facilitating the capacity of empathy is huge because it has the potential of breaking the devastating cycle of violence and will increase any child's social competence. The more satisfying human connections we develop, the richer and more fulfilling our lives, and nothing facilitates the growth of human connections more than the increased capacity for empathy.

· 7 ·

Strategies to Access
the Pain of Social Rejection

*O*verview: *Research has shown that social rejection leads to aggression. Chronic social rejection leads to depleted coping resources, feelings of helplessness, and depression (Williams, 2007). There is no greater curse that can be visited on a child in terms of long-term prognosis than habitual rejection by one's peers. Research has also shown that social rejection impairs the capacity for trust and empathy so the child enters a vicious circle that leads to still further social rejection. Children who are set apart from their peers because of some individual difference endure great suffering. The stories in this chapter are intended to build a bridge of communication that reduces the loneliness and alienation that these youth experience.*

"THE LITTLE BEE WHO STUNG EVERYONE"
(STRATEGY FOR CHILDREN AGES 7 TO 12)

Purpose: *This story was written based on a repetitive theme in the symbolic play of a seven-year-old boy who took the bumblebee puppet and repetitively stung all the other puppets and the therapist as well. This repetitive play continued until I made the interpretation within the metaphor that perhaps the bumblebee stings everyone because he was once stung, probably more than once, and he doesn't want to take the chance of getting stung again. He would rather sting than be stung. Shortly thereafter, he moved on to a different theme in his play but we continued to use the metaphor of the bee "who had been stung one too many times." Many children adopt the stance that the best defense is a good offense. There are, however, negative social consequences associated with this defensive strategy. This story was written to jumpstart therapeutic exploration of the pros and cons of this way of relating to one's social world. Often children sadly compound the insult of social*

rejection by responding in aggressive ways that make it hard for even those who
would befriend them to approach.

The Story

"A long time ago in the beautiful flower gardens at Partridge Park, about forty miles south of London, there lived a little bumblebee that could not stop stinging. She even stung her friends, not to mention the foxes, the peacocks, the horses, the hens and roosters, the people who worked in the gardens, and all the people who came to see and enjoy the beautiful flower gardens. Her friends just couldn't understand it. They tried to talk to her in bee language, but she didn't want to talk about it. Each time they tried, she just flew off and stung someone else. No one knew what to do and most everyone, even those who wanted to be the bee's friends, were getting really mad at the bee.

"One day the bee disappeared and was gone for a long time. Everyone in Partridge Gardens, the gardeners, the visitors, and the animals including the foxes, the rabbits, the peacocks, the squirrels, the chipmunks, and skunks, breathed a sigh of relief and felt much safer. Then one night the bee came back. Everyone was scared that the little bee would start stinging everyone again, but she didn't. The little bumblebee had changed and no one knew why. (Stop here if younger children get restless and are eager to draw. Then summarize the rest of the story before giving "The Storytelling Directives.")

"Finally, one of the little bees, her most trusted friend approached the little bee and said, 'We are so curious about where you went. What happened to you that you have changed so much? You used to sting everyone and now you don't sting anybody. Will you tell us the story?' The little bee was quiet for a long time and then she said, 'Pass the word, I will tell you and all the others tonight in front of the rose bushes.'"

"There was much talk among the people and all the animals. Each one had an idea about where the little bee had gone and what had happened but no one knew for sure. The little bumblebee's closest friends had a strong hunch that the reason she used to sting everyone, including her friends, was that she must have been stung herself in a very hurtful way, maybe more than once. They decided that the little bee must have made up her mind that, from then on, she was going to do the stinging and the hurting before anyone had a chance to sting or hurt her again.

"No one, however, not even the little bee's closest friends, had any ideas about where the little bee had gone and what had changed her so much. So as the sun went down and darkness began to appear, a huge crowd gathered in front of the beautiful rose bushes. The gardeners were there, the visitors who had come to the gardens to enjoy the flowers, some of whom had been stung by the little bee, the peacocks, the rabbits, the squirrels, the horses, and the foxes all gathered in front of the roses and the little bee said, 'Now I will tell you my story.'"

Drawing Directives

"Before the little bee tells her story, close your eyes if you wish, make yourself comfortable and as relaxed as you can, and try to get in your mind a clear picture of the little bee and then draw the little bee as best as you can."

Follow-Up to the Drawing: Some Issues for the Therapist to Consider

1. At what stage of the bee's development is the drawing focused? Does it show the bee before or after the little bee's dramatic change?
2. Is the bee alone in the drawing or in the company of others?
3. If others are included what is their relationship to the little bumblebee? Are they friends? Are they family? Are they enemies?

Questions for the Child

1. Tell me about your drawing.
2. What is the little bee feeling in your picture?
3. What title would you give your picture?
4. Why do you think the little bee stings everyone?
5. What is the bee doing in your picture?
6. Do you think the little bee felt bad about stinging her friends?

Storytelling Directives

"Now the huge crowd that gathered around the rose bushes has grown even larger with the porcupines, deer, and possum among the latecomers joining all the rest of the animals and people. They could hardly wait any longer to hear the bee's story. The little bumblebee said, 'I know you are anxious to hear how I made such a big change. My story has a beginning, a middle part, and an ending. I will start from the beginning. When I first came to Partridge Park, I . . .'" (The child continues.)

Important Issues for the Therapist to Consider

1. How does the child explain the bee's transformation? Is it magical or achieved through persistent efforts?

2. Did the little bee accomplish this change alone or with the help of others?
3. Was there a clear turning point in the little bee's life?

Follow-Up to the Story

1. What title would you choose for your story?
2. Did it take a lot of courage for the bee to tell the story?
3. Was the bee worried when she came back to the garden whether the animals and people would accept her or not?
4. What stopped the little bee from stinging everyone?
5. What can be learned from your story?
6. Do you think the little bee will ever go back to being the "little bee that couldn't stop stinging"? Why?
7. Is there anything the animals and people in the garden could have done earlier that could have helped the bee to change?
8. Do you think the little bee will continue to live in the garden or go someplace else?

Brian's Story (age 9)   "The bee met up with a wise old bee that told the little bee that you don't sting everyone. The wise old bee said you only sting those who frighten you. The little bee was much happier because now she had many more friends and realized that her good friends were right that she had been stinging everyone because she had been stung herself too many times when she was little. Even though she now understood that she had a right to be mad, she did not have the right to sting everyone. The little bee had learned something very important and all the animals and people listening to her story did also."

Anna's story (age 11)   Anna named her picture (see Figure 7.1) "Flying Home." "The little bee is excited because she soon will be home and seeing her friends again. She was stinging people because she had nothing else to do and she was bored. She changed because she has something else to do. She can play with her friends. She learned by watching all the other animals playing together and having fun and realized that she could do this too. Before that she didn't think she could have enough friends even though other bees had tried to be her friend, but she couldn't see it. Now she can and she is much happier."

Directed Symbolic Play with Puppets

The story of the little bee is easily adaptable to puppet play. The bumblebee puppets are two of the most popular puppets in my playroom. One is signif-

Drawing 7.1. "The Little Bee"

icantly smaller than the other and is typically chosen for the part of the little bee. One way to structure the puppet play is to hand the little bee puppet to the child at the point when she is ready to tell her story and then the other puppets, animals and people, can be the audience. The other puppets then can ask questions of the little bee when she finishes her story of how she changed. Another option would be to hand the child the little bee puppet after the child finishes the story and use the other puppets to ask questions. This may be particularly helpful if the child's story is rather meager and needs to be amplified in a non-threatening, playful way.

If the therapist senses the child is anxious and needs considerable prompting in order to extend the dialogue, the use of puppets may introduce an element of playfulness that allows the child to more easily expand on a story that was truncated. It may be helpful also for those children who are disconnected from their affect to take on the voice of the bee and talk about the bee's story in the first person. The affect in most cases will be more accessible when using this Gestalt approach (Oaklander, 1988).

Among the questions that can be asked within the metaphor of the play (through the voice of the other puppets and people) are the following:

1. Did it take a lot of courage for you to come back to the garden?
2. Were you surprised that we wanted to hear your story of how you changed?
3. Do you like it better now that we are no longer afraid of you?
4. Do you think you will make more friends now that you no longer sting everyone?
5. Is there anything we can do to help you as you become the bee that no longer stings everyone?
6. What did you find hardest about making this change?
7. Before you changed did you feel lonely?
8. Did you ever know any other bees that couldn't stop stinging?
9. Are you more afraid now?
10. Are you happier now?

Therapeutic Work with Symbols

The evocative power of symbols can be enlisted by asking the child to pick a symbol to represent the bee when it was "the little bee that couldn't stop stinging" and a symbol to represent the bee after she changed. The child could also be asked to pick a symbol to represent the feelings of the others in the garden toward the bee before and after she changed. The inquiry would consist of pursuing why the child chose a particular symbol in each instance.

Discussion

Anna's and Brian's stories capture a key struggle in many children who because of the defenses they have developed to protect against further hurt are unable to take advantage of opportunities for closeness with others. It is almost as if these children make a pact with themselves that they will never let anyone get close enough that they could be hurt again. Sadly, like the little bee they end up lonely, isolated, and often depressed.

The little bee disappeared and went off by herself and she began to notice that the other animals were having fun with each other and then a "light bulb" went off in the bee's head and she realized, "I can do that." At that point she returned home eager to see her friends. Many children, however, have been hurt so severely, that when they tell the story, the bee does not come back. The little bee is out there somewhere all alone and cut off from others. Anna's story corresponds with positive changes in her school and social adjustment. She is more hopeful and tells a story of hopeful change and transformation based on observing what others do and realizing she was missing out on the fun things in life. The defenses, adopted by children, sometimes become so rigid and automatic that they end up depriving themselves of the social sustenance needed in order to feel that life is worthwhile.

Not only does the theme of this story resonate with many youngsters seen in clinical settings, but through the bee's story, it also explores the child's theory of change, which has been shown to be an important client variable in psychotherapy outcome research.

If the child's theory of how change takes place is not congruent with the approach taken by the therapist, a desired result may be more difficult to obtain.

"MAX: THE BOY WHO SAT ALONE IN THE SCHOOL CAFETERIA" (AGES 7 TO 12)

Purpose: *Many children in their loneliness feel like the boy in the title of this story even if objectively it is not true, it feels that way in their heart. It is extremely painful to believe that you are all alone in the world. Sadly, children who have been hurt and disappointed repeatedly in relationships put up walls and barriers that virtually guarantee their isolation. They often do not notice when the walls are going up nor do they realize they are living in self-constructed prisons. They are protected but the price of protection is to live in exile from others and often their selves. It is not easy to reach such children because the doors to the prison can only be unlocked from the inside and they will not do so until absolutely convinced that it is* *safe to come out or let someone in. (I wish to acknowledge John O'Donohue (1997) for inspiring me to write about walls as a result of his use of the metaphor of "the prisons in which we choose to live.")*

The Story

"Some kids, when they go out on the playground, can find no one who wants to play with them or include them in the games others are playing. They are lonely and sad kids. These same boys and girls often have trouble finding someone to sit with at lunch. Sometimes they sit alone, other times they try to sit with others but are told to sit somewhere else by the children at the table.

"Max was one of those kids, a fourth grader who had no friends. Max is not a bad kid but he has a hard time keeping up in class. Things never came easily for Max. He was also not very good in sports and was almost always the last to be chosen for teams in gym class.

"Another strike against Max was that his family was poor. He needed braces to straighten out his crooked teeth but his family could not afford them. He wore clothes bought by his mother at garage sales and the other kids made fun of him. He was not well-coordinated and when he tripped on something the other students laughed. He was picked on by kids on the bus, especially the afternoon bus that a lot of fifth and sixth graders rode. Max didn't say much. He was quiet and kept to himself. Max was sitting, however, on a powder keg of feelings."

Drawing Directives

"Try to picture Max in your mind. What does he look like? You can include other students if you wish. You can imagine Max in the classroom, on the playground, on the bus or some other place you choose. When you have a clear picture in your mind, please draw it as best you can."

Follow-Up to the Drawing

1. What title would you choose for your picture?
2. Why did you choose the place you did for your drawing?
3. If there are other students in the drawing, who are they and what are their relationships with Max?
4. Why do you think Max has no friends?
5. What advice would you give Max?
6. If you had a chance to talk to Max's classmates, what would you say to them?

Note to Clinicians: If the child is ready to approach the topic directly, the following questions may be useful:

7. Have you known anyone like Max?
8. Can you remember a time when you felt lonely or sad like Max?
9. If so, what helped you get through such a hard time?
10. Have you ever tried to be a friend to a boy or girl who was lonely and sad like Max?

Directives for the Child's Story

"Now, I would like you to put yourself as fully as you can in Max's shoes. Pretend that you can speak for Max and tell the other kids in his class what it is like to be Max. Try to imagine what it would be like to be Max to ride the bus everyday and be picked on, to go out to the playground and have no one to play with, or go to the lunchroom and have no one to sit with. Try to imagine being laughed at when you tripped on something because you are not well-coordinated and to be the last chosen when the class divides into teams. Try to picture yourself coming from a family that was poor in relation to the other kids in the school, your clothes are secondhand, and the other kids make fun of you because your teeth are crooked. Another option is to write a story about Max in which you describe in detail how he feels as he faces rejection each day at school."

Follow-Up

1. What are the main points you would make to the class?
2. What feelings do you think are the most painful for Max?
3. How would you go about helping a kid like Max?
4. What do you think it is like for Max to be teased and bullied on the bus?
5. Which do you think would be worse: (1) to be teased or bullied; or (2) completely ignored by other kids?
6. How do you think Max feels when he goes to bed at night after a hard day at school?
7. How do you think that Max feels when he wakes up on a school day and realizes that he is going to have to face the other kids again today?
8. What do you think adults don't understand or appreciate about sad and lonely kids like Max?

Discussion

In a lecture at Marist College, James Garbarino (2006b) stated, "Social rejection is the closest thing to a psychological malignancy. In every culture children who are socially rejected tend to turn out badly because acceptance is one of the most basic needs of a human being."

All children will be able to identify to some degree with a child like Max. Every youngster has periods of loneliness, sadness, boredom, and social rejection. Kids who face these problems on a chronic basis, however, suffer greatly. Not all youth who suffer the emotional pain of isolation are from low-income families. An increasing number come from middle-class and affluent families. Clinical experience with these youngsters reveals rage because they feel that no one has time for them.

Research shows that neglect is even more devastating than abuse. Kids who are abused typically have periods when they are in relationship with their parents whereas neglected children feel they do not matter enough for parents or caregivers to bother with them.

It is important for children to realize that they can make a real difference in the lives of youngsters who they befriend and that there may come a time in their lives when they will desperately need a friend. Giving to others is therapeutic in a powerful way. Hardy and Laszloffy (2005) explain, "The power of validation through having something to give has taught us that when working with adolescents, especially those prone to violence, it is extremely helpful to identify their capacity for giving. The giving can be almost anything—teaching a younger brother, sister, or neighborhood child how to improve their jump shots, tutoring a fellow classmate in a favorite subject, sharing the wisdom they gained about how to get out of a gang with other adolescents who are still struggling to get out, helping a parent with younger sibling or with chores around the house, picking up groceries for an elderly relative, volunteering at a nursing home or a youth center, or caring for a newly acquired pet. The list of possibilities is limitless" (Hardy and Laszloffy, 2005, p. 175).

What children need that is just as basic and essential as food bought in a grocery store is the emotional nutrients that can't be bought in any store, and no amount of money can ensure—the basic emotional nutrition of love, acceptance, and belonging. These are the greatest gifts that any parent, teacher, therapist, or peer can offer a child, gifts that enrich the child as well as the giver in ways that money can't buy.

"BEHIND CLOSED DOORS" (AGES 9 TO 17)

Purpose: *This story is written for troubled pre-teens and teens who will readily identify with the boy in this story in the principal's office. Jerome, the main charac-*

ter in the story, is a troubled and troubling youth. The adults in his life—including his parents, teachers, and school officials—are about to give up on him and Jerome is also extremely discouraged. Many children in psychotherapy suffer demoralization and the story offers them opportunities to share these feelings within the safety of the metaphor of the story. In addition, the story offers children opportunities to show empathy for Jerome's plight, which will typically reveal a capacity for empathy for self as well as others.

The Story

"Jerome, age twelve, was sitting in the principal's office at Platte City Middle School on a hard-backed, uncomfortable chair, for the twelfth time this school year, and it was only March. He knew that the principal, Mr. Reece, and his teacher, Mr. Pulley, were meeting with his parents. He could hear voices getting louder and louder, but he couldn't make out what they were saying. He knew they were deciding whether he would be suspended for the rest of the year and given home tutoring, or suspended for five days and allowed to continue at school with a one-to-one aide. Jerome didn't much care what they chose behind the closed door because he had given up on school, convinced that everyone at school had given up on him. So, if they decided he couldn't come back to school the rest of the year that was okay with him.

"Jerome was in major trouble after an incident in the hallway that took place in the brief time period between his social studies and science class, around 1:30 p.m. Roberto had been teasing and taunting him all year long and they had been in fights before. In fact, about half of Jerome's visits to Mr. Reece's office resulted from some kind of fight or battle with Roberto. This time, however, it was more serious. Roberto called Jerome an 'idiot' and 'dumb cluck' one too many times and he took a swing at Roberto as they were going down the hall. Jerome missed with his punch, but Roberto didn't. He landed a hard right hook to Jerome's jaw. This not only hurt Jerome but also made him even more furious. He hauled off with a hard right of his own, aimed squarely at Roberto's head, but in the meantime, Mrs. Hansen, who was behind the boys when the fight broke out, stepped between them, hoping to break it up.

"Jerome caught a glimpse of Mrs. Hansen and was able to pull back slightly, but it was too late to stop his fist from landing a blow to the face of Mrs. Hansen, who fell down in great pain. She was lying on the floor, grasping her head with both hands, moaning in pain. Both Jerome and Roberto looked horrified and shocked.

"Almost immediately, a large group converged on the pair and separated them. The security guard and the assistant principal arrived quickly, otherwise there would have been a riot. A huge group of middle-school boys and girls were staring daggers at Jerome. They were outraged that Jerome had hit Mrs.

Hansen, a popular teacher, and were unwilling to consider it an accident. Regardless of how it happened, Mrs. Hansen was lying injured on the floor.

"The security guards and assistant principal moved the group away from the scene, eventually breaking up the group and moving them in the direction of their next class. But not before a number of them shouted at Jerome, 'We are going to get you for this! You are going to pay big time for this.' The principal grabbed Jerome by the arm and escorted him away from the angry crowd.

"The school nurse, Mrs. Reece, the wife of the principal, helped Mrs. Hansen up from the floor and took her to the nursing office. The assistant principal took Roberto with him. Mr. Reece told Jerome on the way to his office that he had really blown it this time and that he would have to wait in the outer office until his parents arrived and a decision was made about what would happen to him.

"About forty-five minutes later, his parents arrived. They were so angry with Jerome that they couldn't even speak to him. Jerome just looked at the floor. He could not look his parents in the eye.

"Jerome's jaw was really hurting, but what hurt a whole lot more was that he had hit and hurt Mrs. Hansen and that no one would ever forgive him for that, even though it had been an accident. He even had thoughts of making a run for it by bolting out the door, but he knew that action would make a bad situation even worse. The principal, Mr. Reece, his teacher, Mr. Pulley, and his parents were still talking loudly, expressing very strong feelings behind the closed door, while Jerome just slumped deeper into his chair."

Drawing Directive

"Now try to get a clear picture of Jerome in mind. You can picture him in the principal's office, in the hallway, during the fight, or anyway you choose. Is he alone or is he with others? Who else is there and what are they doing? When you have a clear picture in your mind, please draw that picture as best you can."

Follow-Up to the Drawing

1. Tell me about your picture.
2. What title would you give to your picture?
3. If others are included, who are they and what is their relationship with Jerome?
4. What is Jerome feeling in your picture?
5. What do you think will be decided behind the closed door?

6. What are the strong feelings that were expressed behind the closed door by Jerome's parents? Mr. Pulley, his teacher? Mr. Reece, the principal?

Storytelling Directives

"Now I want you to pretend that you are Jerome's friend and that you know him better than just about anyone outside of his family. You ask permission to speak with Mr. Reece, Mr. Pulley, and Jerome's parents before the final decision is made. You explain to Mr. Reece's secretary that you have important information that they should know about Jerome. She confers with Mr. Reece and he agrees to let you speak to the group of adults who are meeting about Jerome. Make up a story about what you would tell them about Jerome that is important—information that could influence the final decision about what will happen to Jerome."

Follow-Up to the Story

1. What title would you give your story?
2. After telling your story, do you think the principal and Mr. Pulley might allow Jerome back at school?
3. What was the strongest feeling that Jerome had when he was sitting in the principal's office outside the closed door?
4. What were some of the other feelings he was going through?
5. How do you think things turned out for Jerome in the long run?
6. What was his life like when he became an adult?

Note: For children who no longer need to remain in metaphor, the following questions may be helpful:

6. Have you ever been involved in a situation like Jerome's when you were in a lot of trouble for something that you didn't intend to do?
7. Has anyone ever gone to bat for you or stood up for you the way you did for Jerome?

Mark, a twelve-year-old, was so identified with Jerome's plight that he decided on "Jerome and Me" for the title of his picture (see Drawing 7.2). His story of what he would say in the meeting follows: "Jerome has no patience and he can't control his anger and he can't believe what he did. This other kid, Roberto, is always making fun of him. Jerome is smart; he is fun to be with. He almost always is there to back me up. He is like any other kid; he likes video games, sports, and wrestling."

Drawing 7.2. "Jerome and Me"

When following up Mark's drawing and story, he described Jerome as feeling really embarrassed and upset. He is also lonely because nobody wants to be his friend after this happened. When asked what the decision behind closed doors might be, Mark said that Jerome would be suspended for about two weeks and given another chance, but only one more chance. He described both Jerome's parents and his teacher as shocked by Jerome's behavior, as well as Mr. Reece, the principal, as being "really mad." Mr. Reece can be seen yelling at Jerome's father through the window. In terms of the outcome, Mark thinks that his sticking up for Jerome made a difference and that he convinced the principal and teacher that Jerome could do better and should be given another chance. It is interesting that when making the case for Jerome, Mark made no mention that hitting Mrs. Hansen was an accident. This is probably because impulse-ridden kids like Jerome, with whom Mark closely identified, after experiencing a number of similar incidents, feel that no one is likely to believe that such an action could be an accident, even if true.

When Mark was asked about a time when he got into a lot of trouble for something he didn't intend to do, like Jerome, he described taking a candy bar from a store, when he was very young, perhaps five or six. He said that he didn't think it through and found himself in big trouble. Mark was quite taken with the expression he had drawn on Jerome's face when talking about his own experience of being in trouble. He described Jerome as being "expressionless, like he is in shock, like in a horror movie." Mark said that when he gets into trouble for something he didn't think through that this is exactly how he feels. Mark was able to recall an incident when he got into trouble at school, but another boy took the blame for it. That incident was the only time when he could recall someone going to bat for him the way he stood up for Jerome in the story.

Mark's view of Jerome's long-term future is quite hopeful, paralleling his own turn around, since Mark has made considerable progress in anger control and is now doing well in school. Mark sees Jerome getting a good job in the future after going to college. "He went on to be a wrestler, because in wrestling you can fight and he likes to fight." Mark sees Jerome as still angry and needing to fight, but able to re-channel his feelings in a constructive way while making a living doing it. This is a rather adaptive and creative solution, although one can certainly question the realism of such an outcome.

Discussion

Whenever youth experience shame and stigma, their feelings tend to be shrouded in secrecy. It is very difficult for them to share their feelings with others even in a therapeutic setting. The story is intended to provide middle-school children who have experienced more than their share of social rejection a face-saving way to explore through the safe distance provided by the story these painful feelings. Such kids are sometimes narrowly judged as simply "bad kids." Unfortunately they come to view themselves in the same way and they eventually lose hope.

This projective drawing and storytelling strategy taps into several key issues. It offers opportunities for expressing empathy and understanding for a child in trouble, a situation that many children in treatment easily identify with because of their own experience. It offers an opportunity to practice being helpful to others, a behavior identified through research as important for development of resilience. It also provides an opportunity to assess the child's perception of resources that can be tapped when in major trouble.

Some children will so closely identify with Jerome in the story that they will step out of metaphor to directly discuss their similarly painful social world. Otherwise, therapists are advised to remain within the metaphor. Therapists should pay close attention to the strength and effectiveness of the case the child makes on behalf of Jerome, as well as the affect behind it. Does the child believe that Jerome is worth advocating for or does the appeal on behalf of Jerome seem half-hearted? The effort probably reflects similar attitudes toward the self.

This drawing and storytelling exercise, more than the others in this book, allows for close identification with the central character since many children in treatment have had plenty of experience being in trouble and being sent to the principal's office. Unfortunately, as mentioned previously, children coming to therapy often feel, at least in the beginning, that they are once again in the principal's office, viewing therapy as another punishment. This sense is heightened if the parents have said, "If you don't straighten out, I am going to take you to see a therapist."

HOW THESE STRATEGIES CAN
ENHANCE THE THERAPY PROCESS

The stories in this chapter present through the metaphor of the story characters an opportunity to initiate discussion with children and pre-teens about social rejection, an issue that is extraordinarily sensitive, often associated with shame, embarrassment, and stigma. Even if children never come out of metaphor and relate social rejection to their own personal pain, it can nevertheless reduce their loneliness and isolation by identifying and empathizing with the story characters.

These stories may be even more effective in group therapy where the support of group members can be mobilized further reducing the barriers between the child and others. In addition to creating a safe pathway to explore loneliness and other painful feelings in ostracized children, the stories also build on the strategies in Chapter 6 in providing opportunities and practice in showing empathy for the socially rejected story characters and depending on the degree of their identification with these protagonists, thereby revealing a capacity for empathy for self. Nearly all children have suffered degrees and instances of social rejection, so while the stories will especially be helpful for children who experience chronic social shunning, they will also be useful with children who suffer rejection less often.

Strategies to Address
Grief and Traumatic Loss

*O*verview: *Grief is a human experience and should not be pathologized. Typically children and families turn to their extended families, friends, surrounding community, and in many cases to their religious or spiritual leaders to deal with the anguish of grief. Under some circumstances, grief can be complicated and/or traumatic, and in those instances, intervention by trained child and family clinicians may be needed. The strategies in this chapter are designed to assist clinicians in facilitating grief in children and families when they are called on to help a grieving child and/or family.*

"HELLOS AND GOODBYES" (AGES 6 TO 17)

Purpose: *"Hellos and Goodbyes" is one of the "Heartfelt Feelings Coloring Card Relational Strategies" (HFCCS). "Hellos and Goodbyes" is designed to offer structured opportunities for children to discuss in therapy those people who have recently come into their lives ("The Hellos") as well as those who have departed ("The Goodbyes").*

Background

"Hellos and Goodbyes" was originally described as an evocative strategy to engage children in dialogue about important new relationships as well as the painful loss of other relationships (Crenshaw, 2006b, pp. 39–41). By including it in the HFCCS, therapists do not need to rely on strictly verbal exchange to approach this important issue. The "Hellos" are meant to emphasize that our lives are made richer by the new connections and new relationships we make as we go through life. It is also meant to help the child appreciate the natural cycle of life as new people come into our lives even as others depart. Our life is inevitably made up of many "hellos" and "goodbyes." This series is also a way of stressing that our relationships derive their meaning and specialness partly because of the limited time available to enjoy them. We only have our parents alive for a portion of our lives; we can never take our attachments for granted. The strategy also creates opportunities for important therapeutic conversations centered on the possibilities of growth through suffering.

Directives to the Child: "Hellos"

"Please draw in the heart a picture of a person who has come into your life in the past year that has made a positive difference in your life. It could be a new friend, a new schoolmate, a new neighbor, a new soccer coach, a teacher that has made your life better, fuller, and/or happier. When you have finished your picture, please write a note to the person you picked or tell me the story of why you picked that person." These directions should be repeated until the child can't identify any other "Hellos."

Symbol Work with the "Hellos"

This strategy can be developed further by asking the child to arrange all the "Hello" cards in a circle. Then the child is asked to choose a symbol from a collection of miniatures to represent self and each of the people depicted on the "Hello" cards and to place the symbols on top of the designated card. The therapist can then pursue why the child chose each symbol for each of the persons represented in the "Hello" cards as well as the symbol picked for self. For those children whose social world is rather sparse and who are unable to identify few if any "Hellos," the therapist can modify the instructions to ask the child to include people they like that they have met in soccer, scouts, or church or temple. The therapeutic dialogue may then center on how they can make friends with those they have met and liked.

Directives to the Child for the "Goodbyes"

"'Goodbyes' are usually harder than the 'Hellos.' Sometimes a good friend will move away or simply move on and find new friends and we may feel left behind. A grandparent who is quite old may become extremely sick and die and we feel very sad. Sometimes, but not very often, an accident will happen and there is no time to say goodbye. That can cause a person to be especially sad and sometimes mad or scared. Think about the people this past year that you had to part from or say goodbye to, people you miss, and thinking about them makes you sad. Please draw in your heart one of these persons and then write a note to that person or tell the story of why you picked this person or pet."

These directions can be repeated until the child has the opportunity to do a Relational Card for each of the important "Goodbyes." If the child has not yet encountered the death of someone close, either person or pet, explore the loss of friends, cutoffs with relatives, people moving away, or extend the period beyond the last year.

Symbol Work with the "Goodbyes"

Children who are blocked in their access to their feelings and have not been able to grieve may benefit by picking a symbol from the miniatures to represent self and each of the persons or pets depicted on the "Goodbye" cards. Clinical judgment will be needed as to whether this would be helpful for a particular child at a given time. In general, children who are easily overwhelmed with their feelings would be not good candidates for an emotionally evocative strategy like this. The children more likely to benefit from this strategy are those children blocked in their grief that has resulted in symptoms such as sleep problems or behavioral problems that can be traced back to the death of someone important, particularly if they are unable to talk about it. The power of symbol was dramatically brought home to me when a seven-year-old child who had suffered multiple losses chose symbols for his grandfather, his dog, his pony, two good friends who moved away, a cousin who died, and lined them up at the far end of the room. He picked a little boy with a sad face to represent himself and he was standing at other end of the room, all alone. I asked him what the little boy was feeling and he replied, "He wants them to all come back."

"THE LITTLE PIG THAT DIDN'T FIT" (STRATEGY FOR CHILDREN AGES 7 TO 11)

Purpose: *This story is designed to capture the impact of disrupted attachments and the difficulty of forming new attachments when one is viewed as "the one that simply doesn't fit with the rest." This issue is particularly compelling when children have suffered multiple losses and especially children placed in out-of-home placements. These children almost always feel that they were the ones that "were pushed out of the nest." Often these children have profound difficulties with bonding and* *attachment that make it hard for them to adjust in new foster homes or pre-adoptive families. The issue that the "little pig" in the story struggles with is one that these children will readily identify with—"Do I take the risk of investing in new relationships (family) or do I play it safe, keep my distance because I can't bear to be hurt again?"*

The Story

"Many years ago, on a Northwest Missouri farm, a female pig was born that became known as the Little Pig That Didn't Fit. She was the runt of a group of eight piglets born on December 9, 1961. Her bigger, stronger sibling piglets pushed her aside when it was time for the sow pig to let her piglets suckle. She often felt resentful because she could only receive the mother's milk when her pig brothers and sisters were completely satisfied. Sometimes the little pig would not get the nourishment she needed to grow healthy and strong. As a result, her siblings continued to grow bigger and stronger and she barely held her own, so the gap between her and her sibling piglets got bigger and bigger. Her brother and sister piglets made fun of her, as did all the other pigs on the farm. Farmer Woodson was also getting frustrated. He often would say, 'I can't figure out what is wrong with that little pig, she just doesn't suckle well and all the others are growing bigger and stronger and the little runt is hardly growing.' Farmer Woodson said, 'She just doesn't seem to fit with all the others.' (For restless and younger children stop here and go to Drawing Directives. Summarize the rest of the story before giving the Storytelling Directives.)

"Things did not get any better. In fact, they got worse. The more frustrated that Farmer Woodson became, the more her siblings made fun of her and laughed at her, the less willing she was to do what was expected of her. She didn't seem to care whether she ate the food that Farmer Woodson put in the trough twice a day. She deliberately aggravated Farmer Woodson by digging a tunnel under his fence not only allowing her to get out, but also leaving enough space for other pigs to get under the fence. This made Farmer Woodson mad. He would often yell out, 'I don't know what I am going to do with that runt pig; she just doesn't fit with the others.' The other pigs picked up this theme and would sometimes mock the little pig and chant all together, 'You are a runt, you don't belong, and you don't fit with the rest of us.'

"One night, after another long day of using her snout to root underneath the fence, the little pig escaped under the fence, but this time she only dug deep enough to let herself out. In fact, the other pigs didn't even notice that she was gone. When Farmer Woodson came to feed the pigs that next morning, he also didn't notice that the little pig was no longer there.

"The little pig traveled a long distance and she was now tired and hungry. When her little legs got so heavy she could hardly take another step, she was startled by a little girl's voice, 'Oh Daddy, look at the cute little pig.' Farmer Pratt stared at the little pig and said, 'Well, I declare, that must be the little runt pig from Farmer Woodson's farm. He is always talking about that little pig that doesn't fit with all the rest.' 'Oh Daddy,' said the little girl, whose name was Judy, 'but she is so cute! Can we keep her, Daddy?' 'Oh no, Judy, I have to call Farmer Woodson right away; he is probably looking for his little pig.' Judy was heartbroken. Farmer Pratt and his wife had horses and cows on their small farm but no pigs. Judy thought the pig was so cute and would fit right in with the horses and cows on the farm.

"Farmer Pratt was quite surprised when he called Farmer Woodson that he didn't even know the little pig was missing and didn't seem concerned about it. He said to Farmer Pratt, 'That little runt has been a nuisance ever since she was born and she just doesn't fit in with the other pigs, would you like to keep her?' Farmer Pratt was not expecting this and didn't know what to say, but knowing how happy it would make Judy, his little girl, he finally said, 'Well sure, if that's what you want, we'll keep her.' When Judy heard that, she let out screams of pure joy, jumped up and down, and hugged her dad and mom. Her parents had never seen Judy so excited and happy. Judy ran out to the fenced in area around the barn and gave the little pig a big hug. Judy picked her up and squeezed her with all her heart. The little pig had never been picked up or hugged before and didn't know what to make of it. In fact, it scared her and she started wiggling, squirming, and screaming loudly. Judy put the little pig down and she went running off to a dark corner of the fenced pen. The little pig was uncomfortable with the very thing she always wanted. The little pig was confused. She always wanted to be hugged, to be loved, to feel special, and to belong. Now the little pig had what she always wanted, but perhaps she didn't feel she deserved it. Maybe she couldn't trust it; maybe she was afraid that something would change or go wrong at Farmer Pratt's farm and that, once again, she would be the Little Pig That Didn't Fit.

"The little pig was puzzled by how uneasy she felt. She asked herself, 'Why am I not happy?' Judy and her parents make me feel so special and, yet, I feel like I don't belong.' It just didn't make any sense. The only place that she felt comfortable was in the place where she didn't fit. Slowly and sadly, she began to move in the direction of Farmer Woodson's place. She kept going for a long time, using her talented snout to dig tunnels under fences that she needed to cross. Finally, weary and tired, she came to the fence that separated Farmer Woodson's from Farmer Pratt's property. She knew that if she dug a hole under the fence, she would be back in the place that she didn't fit, but where she felt most comfortable. She hesitated because trying to figure out what to do was not easy for her. She could go back to Farmer Pratt's place where she was treated so well and everyone had tried hard to help her feel special, but the more they tried the more uncomfortable she felt."

Drawing Directives

"Now try to get as comfortable and relaxed as you can. You may close your eyes, if you wish, and try to get a picture of the *Little Pig That Didn't Fit.* When you are ready, please draw as best you can a picture of the *Little Pig That Didn't Fit.*"

Follow-Up to the Drawing

1. Tell me about your drawing.
2. Tell me about the others in the picture (if applicable) and their relation to the Little Pig That Didn't Fit.
3. What title would you give your picture?
4. What is the little pig feeling in your picture?
5. In your picture is the little pig at Farmer Woodson's or at Farmer Pratt's place?

Storytelling Directives

"Now, I would like you to think about the problem the Little Pig That Didn't Fit has to solve. She has to decide whether to go back to the Woodson's farm, where she never fit but felt comfortable or she can decide to go back to the Pratt farm, where she was made to feel welcome but couldn't feel comfortable. Make up a story about the little pig that includes the actual choice she made, what problems came up for her on the farm she chose to go back to, and how it worked out in the long run for the little pig."

Follow-Up to the Story

1. What would be a good title to your story?
2. Why do you think the little pig felt comfortable in the place where she was not treated well?
3. Why do you think the little pig didn't feel comfortable in the place where she was treated nicely?
4. What can be learned from your story?
5. If your story didn't include how things worked out for the little pig in the long run, how do you think it turned out for the little pig?

Note: If the child initiates direct discussion of not belonging outside of metaphor, the following questions may be useful:

1. Does the story of *The Little Pig That Didn't Fit* remind you of anyone?
2. Have you ever felt that you didn't fit or belong? If so, what was that experience like for you?
3. What advice would you give to anyone who feels that /she doesn't fit or belong?

Drawing and Story by Elizabeth (age 11)   "The little piglet will go back to farmer Pratt's place where they tried so hard to help her feel she belonged. Eventually they get more pigs and then the little pig no longer feels so special and is able to feel more comfortable." (See Drawing 8.1.)

Discussion

Elizabeth's story succinctly captures a key dynamic for children with significant attachment problems. This story, like the *Misunderstood Mouse*, with a theme of "not fitting in" or "not belonging" goes to the heart of the conflict experienced by children with attachment disorders or those who fear intimacy. Children in the foster care system, those with frequent disruptions of early relationships, have profound difficulties with bonding and attachment. Like the little pig in Elizabeth's story, many of these children do better in group-care than in family settings because of fewer demands for intimacy and closeness.

Drawing 8.1.   "The Little Piglet"

When other pigs were added to the farm, the little pig no longer felt so special and could feel more comfortable. For children with attachment disorders, it is a tremendous strain to relate in the intimate manner expected within families. The prospect of closeness, longed for at one level, is also feared, if not terrifying. This core conflict has been referred to as a "crisis of connection" (Crenshaw, 1995). Frequently, these children will sabotage relationships when closeness starts to develop as a result of the anxiety aroused by the threat of intimacy. The sabotage may take the form of acting-out behavior or running away. When they run away, they are running from the warmth the attachment figures offer, warmth they have always longed for, but are too frightened to trust.

Although children with attachment disorders are disorganized emotionally by the prospect of closeness, paradoxically, they are also sensitive to any threat of separation or loss. This makes sense when you consider that many of the children have suffered multiple losses. Typically, the children do not reveal their feelings about loss and perhaps do not even acknowledge their losses to others, or even to themselves, but if a shift in the environment occurs, which threatens separation or loss, the children react intensely. During my years in residential treatment, I was amazed by how often a child made a suicidal gesture after a particular childcare worker or teacher went on vacation or was absent from work or when the child's family underwent some change.

When parents separate, the fear of many children is that they will have no place, that they will not fit in or belong in the parents' new lives. These issues of attachment and loss, acknowledged or, as is often the case, unacknowledged, are powerful issues that can easily be overlooked by those not working within a family systems orientation. In contrast, when working within a family systems orientation, whenever you meet with a child or a family, the question in the back of your mind should always be, "Who is not here, or no longer here, who was once important to this child?"

"THE MAGIC KEY"

One of the Projective Drawing Strategies, *The Magic Key* (Crenshaw, 2004; Crenshaw and Mordock, 2005), was developed to evoke themes of loss, longing, and missing in the lives of children. The instructions, however, have been modified from the original strategy as shown below:

"Imagine that you have been given a magic key that opens one room in a huge castle. There are four floors in the castle and since the castle is huge there are many rooms on each floor, but your magic key only opens one of the many, many rooms in the castle. So pretend you go from room to room and from floor to floor, trying your magic key in each door until you finally come to the door that your key opens. You turn the key and the lock opens. Because this is a magic key that only opens this door, what you see is the one thing that has always been missing from your life—the one thing you always believed would make you happy that money can't buy. Pretend that you are looking into the room. What is it that you see? What is that one thing that has been missing that you always believed would make you happy that money can't buy? When you have a clear picture, please draw it as best you can."

The original instructions didn't include the caveat "that money can't buy." Consequently, not surprisingly in this highly consumer-oriented culture, children often drew a big screen or flat panel TV. The children, however, who didn't draw the latest consumer gadget often depicted something quite meaningful and often poignant such as a missing or deceased parent, a safe home they never experienced, or a family where the parents don't argue so often. They drew a home they always longed for, one which is sadly missing in their lives. This projective drawing strategy can be useful with children whose lives are replete with loss. Many severely aggressive children have suffered profound, multiple losses. The value of this projective drawing is that it sometimes brings into focus for both the child and therapist the losses that the child had not previously acknowledged. Sometimes this is because the nature of the loss is too painful to acknowledge and in other cases either the cognitive awareness or the affect associated with the loss has been dissociated (Hardy and Laszloffy, 2005). In the latter case, the child may speak of a death of a brother in the same matter-of-fact way they would discuss the scores of a ballgame. The grief is disconnected from the cognitive awareness of the loss. In the former instance, a youth may experience sadness or rage but be unaware cognitively of its association to the painful loss or losses they have suffered. In fact, the Freudian notion of making the unconscious conscious in therapy is now seen by Bromberg (1998) and other seminal thinkers (Darwin, 2007) as making the dissociated associated.

The therapeutic task becomes one of bringing the disavowed affect states into awareness where these states can be integrated. This strategy can assist in this process because an important aspect of the work with these youngsters is to help them move from unacknowledged grief to acknowledged (Hardy and Laszloffy, 2005). It is sometimes quite a surprise for a youngster who draws the father who has never been a part of his or her life in that room "that the magic key opens." Father absence is frequently minimized especially by male children. Boys often insist, "He was never a part of my life and I don't miss him." As long as the loss is denied or unacknowledged, the grief process can't begin. When they discover that they had drawn their father in the room, they can appreciate that this loss has meant more to them than they realized or were able to admit. This is an important first step in the healing process.

Many children with unacknowledged loss experience rage but are unaware that the rage is a result of their unmourned losses. One twelve-year-old child drew a "safe home" in the room. This child, who was referred by his school for aggressive behavior at school, had witnessed domestic violence but *The Magic Key* opened the door for him to talk in more depth about what he had witnessed, but even more importantly it enabled him to express his rage within the therapeutic setting and to realize for the first time that beneath the rage was tremendous sorrow that he did not live in a "safe home."

"THE 'LINKING OBJECT' INTERVENTION" (STRATEGY FOR CHILDREN AGES 9 TO 17)

Purpose: *This intervention is based on the writing of Vamik D. Volkan (1981). Volkan, a psychoanalyst, defines a linking object as "the externalized version of an introject" (Volkan, 1999, p. 172). He explains, "The mourner 'chooses' an external item such as the watch of his dead father, and psychologically speaking, makes it magical. This linking object unconsciously connects the lost person's image or mental representation with the mourner's corresponding self-image or representation. It becomes a psychological meeting ground for both" (Volkan, 1999, p. 172). Volkan distinguishes between a linking object and what he calls a linking phenomenon. Volkan states, "A linking phenomenon refers to a song, a smell, a gesture, an action, or an affect that functions as a linking object" (Volkan, 1999, p. 173). The intervention described based on Volkan's concepts are primarily focused on the goal of helping children and teens to gain access to their blocked or delayed affect that has prevented them from proceeding with grieving and mourning. This intervention because of its evocative power should only be used in the context of a strong therapeutic alliance and with children who are unable to access their emotional life following the death of someone important to them.*

Children and teens who are able to directly embrace their feelings would not need an intervention like this and it could be contraindicated since they might feel overwhelmed by the powerful emotional stimulus. Compared to the other strategies in this book, I refer to this particular strategy as an intervention because it requires greater skill and experience on the part of the therapist and it is not recommended for new and inexperienced therapists unless done under the careful supervision of a highly experienced clinician.

It is recommended that other strategies to facilitate the expression of the child's affect be used first. Strategies commonly used by therapists and grief counselors to enable children to access their feelings include asking about their favorite memories and their favorite stories of their loved one, and special times spent with their loved one. Some children, particularly younger ones, can access their affect easier when asked to draw their favorite memory or a special time with their loved ones. Images are more powerful than words in bringing affect into awareness and allowing children to experience it directly in the context of a healing and trusting relationship with their therapist.

Sometimes a memory album of favorite photographs or pictures that the children draw depicting their favorite memories and times serves both the purpose of enabling children to connect with their emotions as well as to commemorate and honor their loved one (Crenshaw, 1990, [1995], [2002], 2005, 2006a, 2007b; Worden, 1996). Symbols can assist children in expressing the emotions of grief as well. I will sometimes ask children to pick a symbol to represent their loved ones and then inquire as to why they picked that particular symbol for their deceased loved ones. Another variation is to ask children to pick a symbol from a group of miniatures to represent self before and after the death of their loved ones. This can sometimes powerfully depict the devastation the child feels such as when a eight-year-old boy whose father was killed in a car accident depicted through miniatures (symbols) playing catch with his father and after the death standing alone and feeling lost.

The use of the *Linking Object* is indicated when the other more typical interventions have failed to allow children to connect with their emotional life and are blocked in their emotional expression of their grief.

Directions to the Child and/or Family

Because of the evocative emotional power of this intervention, I strongly prefer to do it with the participation of the child's family who are prepared ahead of time and are in agreement with the plan for the intervention. In a family session, I will ask each member of the family if is there some object at home or in their possession that strongly links them to their deceased loved family member. I often give the example of a coffee mug with the St. Louis Cardinals emblem that my grandfather always drank from when he had his morning coffee. After my grandfather died, whenever I visited my grandmother and saw that coffee mug in the cabinet, I felt a strong and powerful emotional link with my grandfather, almost as if he were in the room drinking his morning coffee. Then I ask, "Is there some object like that for each of you that link you in an emotional way with your loved one?" Usually each family member is able to come up with one or more objects. Sometimes several family members will pick the same linking object. Then we discuss why these objects have acquired such magical linking powers for each of the family members. This is typically a highly emotional session and often in the healing presence of the surviving family sharing together their grief it is an important step in enabling the blocked child to gain access to the buried grief.

At the end of the session, the family members are asked if they would be willing to bring in their linking objects for the next session. In the case of a family member picking a particular rocking chair or some other object in the home that is not easily portable, I raise with the family the possibility of having the next session in their home. Whenever this has arisen, the family, without exception, has been willing to have the session in their home and it has greatly enhanced the powerful emotional impact of this intervention. Sitting in the living room with the family at the child's grandmother's house and looking at the empty easy chair that grandpa always sat in while watching TV and reading the newspaper has been not only a deeply moving experience for the family but for me as the therapist as well.

Discussion

When the session is held in the office, the most frequent objects brought in are photographs, pieces of jewelry, watches, coffee mugs, caps, coats, pocket knives, and sweaters. I ask family members to hold in their lap their linking object and to take turns talking about the link to their loved one, associated memories and happy times.

In my clinical experience, it has typically been boys more than girls who are unable to access their emotions of grief, but not always. One other variation I have used if the above intervention does not allow access to the blocked emotions of grief, is to bring in an empty chair (a Gestalt technique) and to put the linking object on the empty chair beside them and ask them to look at it while describing the link to the loved one. This is particularly evocative and helpful for those children who are extremely cut off from their feelings.

This is not intended to be an isolated dramatic intervention but rather to be integrated in an ongoing therapeutic process where timing and pacing must carefully be considered and a close alliance has been established between child and therapist as well as therapist and family. The follow-up is equally important since just releasing the feelings without allowing for working through or integrating the powerful emotions of grief would be potentially harmful. It is important that therapists using this intervention have specific knowledge and training, as well as experience in grief work, due to the intensity of emotional abreaction that can be expected.

Clinical Illustration

One of the unforgettable moments in my therapy career took place in a family session when I used the "linking object" intervention. The eight-year-old child was trying "to outrun his affect," in contrast to his ten-year-old sister who was able to grieve quite openly along with her mother for her deceased father. The boy was trying to "outrun" his emotions by constant motion, never able to sit still in his classroom at school or in his therapy sessions. His teacher was so convinced that he had ADHD that she talked the mother into taking him to his pediatrician who put him on Ritalin. The Ritalin did not help because ADHD was not the problem. I came to understand that this child was afraid to sit still long enough that he would feel the impact of the death of his father who was a fireman who died in the World Trade Center terror attack. After all of my more typical strategies to facilitate the grief of children had failed to help this child access his emotional life, we did a family session. His mother brought their wedding picture; his sister, Kelly, brought a stuffed animal that her father had given her for her fourth birthday and has been cherished ever since; and Tommy brought in his Dad's fire hat. It was a powerful and evocative picture of each of them holding their cherished link to their loved one, but it wasn't until I asked Tommy to put his Dad's fire hat on the empty chair and look at it while telling us what it meant to him that the dam finally broke and the long denied and blocked tears were given expression as his mother and sister cuddled him. That was a beginning: it took many more sessions in follow-up to help him integrate these powerful feelings, but three months later, no one, including his teacher, saw him as ADHD because he was no longer trying to "outrun his feelings."

Please note: I have designated this intervention to be used with pre-adolescents and adolescents. Obviously, the child in the above illustration was younger and sometimes this intervention can be used with younger children but would depend on clinical judgment and many other factors such as strength of the therapeutic alliance, degree of family support and resources, child's internal strengths and resources, timing, and pacing.

Additional Options

If the child is too anxious or threatened to benefit from the above intervention, it is possible to create further symbolic distance that may enable such youngsters to work with the "linking object" in a meaningful way. The child or teen could be invited to draw the linking object or to pick a symbol from a collection of miniatures to represent the linking object if it is too emotionally difficult to bring the actual object into the session. Alternatively, the family together could collaborate on the drawing or the symbol work. The use of this additional layer of symbolization will also be helpful if the linking object is of a nature, such as an "easy chair," that it is impractical to bring it to the session and for some reason it is not possible to hold the session at home.

HOW THESE STRATEGIES CAN
ENHANCE THE THERAPY PROCESS

The *Hellos and Goodbyes* has a wider application because children who are not necessarily blocked in their grief but need some degree of facilitation of their grief will benefit from this strategy. *The Little Pig That Didn't Fit* also has broad application for assisting children with attachment problems or children who because of some individual difference don't fit in their family or social group to talk about the associated feelings in the less threatening forum created by metaphor and story.

The *Linking Object* by contrast, should be reserved for children suffering traumatic grief or who are blocked or disconnected from their affect but are judged to be clinically ready for an emotionally evocative intervention. As with so many of the techniques presented throughout this book, the use of symbol and artistic depictions can be powerfully facilitative of children and teens gaining access to their emotions thereby enabling them to share them in supportive and empathic therapeutic context. These strategies are examples of many others that can be used for this purpose, some of which were mentioned earlier in the chapter such as creation of memory books, drawing favorite memories, and sharing special stories about their loved ones. Because grief and loss issues tend to be so painful for children, ways of structuring the therapeutic context to make it easier for them to identify, access, and share their feelings become especially valuable.

·9·

The "Quest for Home" Strategies

*O*verview: *Seeking a home, not necessarily a physical home, but a psychological or spiritual home by those who never experienced a secure sense of home early in life, is a common and powerful theme in therapy. These strategies were developed based on the theoretical groundwork established in a book chapter titled, "Seeking a Shelter for the Soul" (Garbarino and Crenshaw, in press), which focuses on the unrequited longing of those who missed out on a "secure base" (Bowlby, 1980) in early life. The theme is also found in literature in the novels, for example, of Steinbeck, Faulkner, and Thomas Wolfe. When this theme is a central preoccupation for children, it brings to mind Maslow's famous statement, "Men don't live by bread alone, unless there is no bread."*

THE THEME OF SEEKING A HOME:
"THIS BUNNY IS LOST AND CAN'T FIND ITS MOTHER"
(STRATEGY FOR CHILDREN AGES 6 TO 9)

Purpose: *This strategy and the ones that follow for different age levels are focused on a powerful theme in therapy of seeking a secure home, a place of refuge. The strategies are intended to approach the sensitive and critical issue of the child's or adolescent's relationships to family and home. The theme is explored through the metaphors and symbols of storytelling with the modest but important goal underlying all the strategies in this book to initiate or expand the therapeutic dialogue with children and teens about heartfelt feelings and meaningful issues that really matter in their lives. Since the remaining strategies in this chapter are developed around this theme with the same purpose and goal, the discussion section will follow the last of the strategies in this group.*

131

Clinical Considerations

Children who long for a "home," especially spiritually and psychologically "homeless" children, will often find it easier to approach this sensitive issue through the symbolic safe haven provided by the metaphors of the "Lost Bunny," "The Puppy Needing a Home," "The House on the Outside/Inside," "The House of Hopes, Dreams, and Promises" and finally the story of "The Secret Life of Nicole." Younger and more vulnerable children in particular may need the shelter of symbolism to approach this topic. Clinical judgment will be needed as to timing of introducing these strategies to a given child, and there will be no substitute for the therapist's knowledge of the strengths and vulnerabilities of the individual child. It is recommended that the therapist remain in the metaphor unless the child or teen initiates direct discussion of the issue.

Some children may find this issue so threatening that they are not able at a given point in time to approach it even using the indirect approach afforded by metaphor and symbol. It is important to honor the defenses of children and not press if any of these strategies create anxiety to the point that the child wishes to discontinue. The child can simply be told, "We can come back to this at another time when it is more comfortable for you." So many children we see in clinical settings are suffering from important losses and disappointments, and many are seeking the "home of their longing," having missed out on that nurturing, safe beginning in life that leads to trust and a sense of security in the world. These children are suffering "psychological" or "spiritual homelessness" (Hardy, 2000; Crenshaw and Garbarino, 2007; Garbarino and Crenshaw, in press). This will especially be true of children in the foster care system who often leave behind a trail of broken attachments as they are admitted into care

Figure 9.1.   Clip Art Picture of the Bunny

Directives to the Child

The child is told the following: "This rabbit is lost, tired, and hungry. The little rabbit has been looking for its mother and can't find her. The bunny is sad and confused." Ask the child to make up a story about what happens to the bunny. In the story the child is instructed to tell whether the bunny finds its mother or not.

Follow-Up to the Story

1. What would be a good title for your story?
2. What can be learned from your story?
3. What does the bunny do to take care of itself while looking for its mother?
4. Does any other animal try to help the bunny?
5. What was the strongest feeling that the bunny had when it could not find its mother?
6. What do you think its mother felt when she realized the bunny was lost?

Use of Symbols

The child can be invited to pick a symbol to represent the bunny and its mother. The therapist explores the choices of symbols. A symbol can also be chosen for the feelings of the bunny and the feelings of the mother.

THEME OF SEEKING A HOME: "THE PUPPY IN THE ANIMAL SHELTER" (PRE-ADOLESCENTS, AGES 9 TO 12)

Purpose: *Since this story involves a puppy that tends to be more central to the lives of most children than a bunny, this story may be more threatening than the previous one and thus is reserved for pre-teens. Also, children who have histories of significant loss will find this story touches on some very tender and sensitive parts of their emotional life.*

Directives to the Child

"This dog was turned into the animal shelter and is waiting for a new home. Please write or tell the story of what went wrong in this dog's previous home. Also, in your story tell what happens to the dog. Is he adopted by a new family? If so, tell in your story what happens to the dog in the new home."

Figure 9.2.   Clip Art of Puppy

Follow-Up to the Story

1. What title would you choose for your story?
2. What can be learned from your story?
3. Why do you think some pet owners give up their pets or abandon them?
4. Do you think there is an important difference between pet owners who try to find a good home for their pet as compared to those who just abandon the animals?
5. Why do you think some pets have a hard time adjusting to a new home?
6. Why do you think pets that have been in several different homes have an especially hard time feeling comfortable in a new home?
7. What can the new family do to make the new pet comfortable and feel safe in their home?
8. Do you think there are some pets that won't be able to accept the new home even if the family is very nice? If so, why do you think so?
9. If you could give advice to the children in the new family about how they could help the dog feel welcome in her new home, what would you tell them to do?

Symbol Work

The child can be asked to pick a symbol for the dog and a symbol for the prior home(s) the pet had lived in and a symbol for the new family. The child can also be invited to pick a symbol for the feelings of the dog in the prior home(s) and/or her feelings in the new home. Likewise, the child can pick symbols to represent the feelings of the prior owner(s) and the new family. This use of symbols allows for further exploration of this potentially threatening issue while remaining in the metaphor.

Drawing

Children may also be invited to draw a picture of the dog in her new family. This may reinforce via the symbolic depiction that regardless of the dog's past, she can make a new start.

THEME OF SEEKING A HOME: "NOT ALL HOMES ARE AS HAPPY ON THE INSIDE AS THEY APPEAR ON THE OUTSIDE." (STRATEGY FOR AGES 12 TO 17)

Purpose: *Sadly, some families carry destructive secrets. In some families it may be alcoholism or drug abuse that ravages the family or compulsive gambling or domestic violence or abuse of the children and yet to the outside world the family may appear perfectly normal. This is because all the family members are enlisted in a conspiracy of silence. Silence is a central dynamic in oppression of any kind and the reason that some children suffer long before authorities become aware and intervene in the situation. This strategy is focused on the theme of destructive secrets and what may go on beyond closed walls. Again, clinicians need to be careful not to overinterpret because children may or may not be hinting about their own home. As stated previously, they may simply like to tell a good "horror story." Typically, over time adolescents will reveal the true nature of their situation by dropping redundant clues. It is from such repetitive themes and patterns in their stories and other communications that we are likely to get a more accurate picture of their life at home.*

Story Directives

"Write or tell a story about the family that lives in this house. Let's pretend that this is an unhappy family but they try to hide it from their neighbors. What is the family's life like on the inside of the home? Are there secrets in

Figure 9.3.   Clip Art of First Home

this family? If you could be a fly on the wall inside the house, what would you observe?"

Follow-Up to the Story

1. What title would you give your story?
2. What can be learned from your story?
3. Does anyone outside the family realize what is going on?
4. If it were possible to observe the family as they really are, what signs would you look for to show that they are unhappy?
5. What kind of secrets are burdens for kids to keep?
6. What advice would you give the children in this family?
7. What advice would you give the parents in this family?
8. How do you think things will turn out in the long run for this family?

Follow-Up Relational Questions

1. Who in this family is most upset?
2. Who in the family can the children go to when they are worried?
3. If the family is keeping secrets, who in the family has the hardest time keeping the secrets?

4. Who in the family would be most angry if the secrets were told?
5. Who in the family is coping best with their unhappy situation?
6. If the children can't turn to their parents, who else could they go to for help?
7. Do you think the children can turn to each other in this difficult family situation?
8. Do you think the kids would turn to their friends for help?
9. What adults outside the immediate family do you think could help the most?
10. Are there any circumstances that you think should lead the kids to go tell their neighbors?

Symbol Work

To further the therapeutic dialogue about this key theme, adolescents can be asked to pick a symbol from a collection of miniatures to represent the family or home as seen from the outside and as it really is on the inside. Inquiry about the selection of the symbols and the disparity between inside/outside symbols may lead to further meaningful exchange while remaining in the metaphor. In addition, the adolescent can be asked to pick a symbol for each member of the family as they appear on the outside and how they really are inside the home.

Drawing

Those teens who find drawing appealing can be invited to draw a picture of the family as seen on the outside and a picture of the family as they really are inside the house. This becomes another useful portal of entry for some teens to access feelings related to a potentially emotionally laden issue.

THEME OF SEEKING A HOME: "HOUSE OF HOPES, DREAMS, AND PROMISES"(STRATEGY FOR CHILDREN AGES 11 TO 17)

Purpose: *Children are more similar than different when it comes to hopes and dreams for the future. When they are young, regardless of whether inner city or rural poor or affluent suburban, they dream and hope to be a NFL, NBA, WBA, or major league baseball player; a doctor; or lawyer. The opportunities, however, for pursuing and fulfilling these hopes and dreams vary widely. By the time some children reach adolescence they are no longer sure they will even live to see adulthood. They encounter many obstacles to reaching their intended and hoped for destination.*

Figure 9.4.   Clip Art of Second Home: "The House of Hope, Dreams, and Promises"

This is especially true for minority youth in the inner cities. The promise of a better life and a future for many of these young people is broken along with crushed hopes and shattered dreams. This strategy is intended to focus adolescents on their hopes, dreams, as well as broken promises and disappointments.

The House of Hopes, Dreams, and Promises Fantasy

"Now I would like you to imagine that you are touring a house that contains in separate rooms your hopes, dreams, and promises for the future. You come to the first room and it is called the Room of Hopes. Please write in the room as many hopes as you can for the kind of life you would like to have in the future.

"Then you come to the next room and this is the Room of Dreams. Write in the box that outlines this room your dreams for the future even if you think they are unlikely to come true, since dreams are important to everyone even though we may be only able to fulfill some of them—perhaps none of them, and almost certainly we will not be able to reach all of them.

"Next we come to the Room of Promises. Promises made to you by your family, your friends, or your teachers or others who along the way have shown a desire to help you. Write in this room some of the important promises that have been made by others to help you reach your dreams and hopes.

"As we continue our tour of the house, the next room we come to is the Barrier Room. This room contains all the barriers and obstacles that you can imagine that stand in the way of your achieving your hopes and dreams of the future. Examples of barriers may include: lack of money, lack of support or encouragement, learning or educational challenges, or anything that you can

■ROOM OF _____

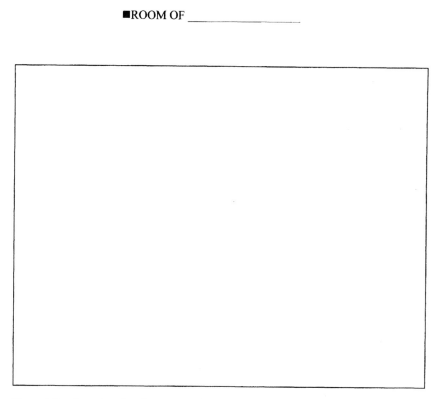

Figure 9.5.   Template for the Rooms of the House

think of that will make it difficult for you to reach your goals of a better life for the future. Write as many of them as you can imagine in the outline of the Barrier Room.

"Finally we come to the Room of Broken Promises and Disappointments. In everyone's life there are disappointments to face, dreams that have to be given up, and in some cases broken promises. Write these in the outline of the room."

Symbol Work with the House of Hopes, Dreams, and Promises

This strategy can be further expanded by inviting teens to pick one or more symbols from the collection of miniatures to place in each of the rooms and to explore their choices in each instance. For those youngsters who have already suffered more than their share of disappointments (real or perceived) this may further elicit the associated affects that can then be explored in the therapeutic interaction.

THEME OF SEEKING A HOME:
"THE SECRET LIFE OF NICOLE"
(STRATEGY FOR PRE-TEENS AND TEENS AGES 12 TO 17)

Purpose: Teens sometimes secretly bear untenable emotional burdens in their families. They dare not tell anyone because of shame. They not only carry a heavy load but they feel stigmatized by it. This story is meant to open up a dialogue with teens about a topic that is often too sensitive for them to directly discuss.

The Story

"Nicole was seventeen and an exceptionally pretty girl, a good student, but quite shy. She didn't attend social events connected with her high school and she did not participate in sports or after school clubs or activities. In fact, most students at her high school didn't really know much about her. Nicole considered three other girls at school to be good friends but not even her friends Michelle, Julie, and Lynn really knew her well. Nicole rarely accepted invitations to their homes and they were not invited to her home.

"Nicole was always pleasant, nice, generous, and loyal as a friend but she never confided in her friends. They assumed she was simply shy. At Plattsville High School, where Nicole was in her junior year, she was regarded as a mystery by most of her teachers and classmates.

"One of her teachers, Mrs. Rice who taught English Literature, was quite concerned by Nicole's secretive nature and her lack of social participation in school activities. She also noticed that in spite of the sweet smile and pleasant face there were subtle signs of sadness, especially in her eyes. Over several months she made a determined attempt to engage Nicole and to get to know her better."

"Mrs. Rice asked Nicole if she would help her with the drama club. Nicole was pleased to be asked but was reluctant to commit to it. Mrs. Rice persisted, however, and finally Nicole agreed. When the drama club ran late causing Nicole to miss her bus, Mrs. Rice offered to drive her home. On the rides to Nicole's home, Mrs. Rice little by little gained Nicole's confidence and began to learn a little more about what Nicole's life outside of school was like.

"Nicole over the course of the rest of the school year was able to tell her story in small bits to a teacher who went out of her way to take a special interest in her and became to Nicole an adult she knew that she could trust. Nicole had never experienced in her family life adults she could rely on. Her mother suffered severe bouts of depression and many mornings never got out of bed. She would sometimes still be in bed when Nicole returned from school.

"Her father worked in a factory but often did not get home until later in the evening because he would hang out in a favorite bar on the way home with his work buddies. When he did arrive home he would expect Nicole to prepare him dinner and he would sometimes get angry with her if he didn't think the house was clean enough or some other thing did not suit him in his often intoxicated state. This was the secret life of Nicole and the heavy burdens she carried everyday that she was ashamed for anyone else to know."

Drawing Directives

(This step is optional. The story may elicit sufficient anxiety in some teens that they will welcome working with this story in the symbolic realm, while others will reject this option.)

"Please try to get an image in your mind of Nicole at home with her family. When you are able to picture her and her family, please draw it as best you can."

Follow-Up to the Drawing

1. Tell me about your picture.
2. What title would you give your picture?
3. What do you think Nicole is feeling in your picture?
4. If you were Nicole's friend and she confided in you about her family life, what advice would you give her?
5. Why do you feel that Nicole feels shame?
6. Have you known of anyone like Nicole who faced difficult family problems that they tried to keep secret?
7. Have you known a teacher like Mrs. Rice who made a special effort to get to know Nicole and help her?
8. What about the sadness that Mrs. Rice noticed in Nicole, do you think others could have picked up sooner on the fact that Nicole was hurting?

Directives for the Story

"Now I would like you to pick up the story of Nicole from the place that it ended. After Mrs. Rice gains Nicole's confidence and learns of the burdens that she secretly carries, please make up a story about what happens to Nicole from there. Do things change for Nicole and her family? What does Nicole do? Does she change and become more involved with her friends and school life or does she continue to protect and take care of her family? What does Mrs. Rice do to help? Does her family make any changes? Who else would you include in your story that might be able to help Nicole and/or her family?"

Follow-Up to the Story

1. What title would you give to your story?
2. What can be learned from your story?
3. How common do you think Nicole's situation is among the teens you know?
4. What do you think adults need to understand about teens like Nicole?
5. How do you think Nicole's life will turn out in the long run?
6. Do you think it was only shame that kept Nicole from telling others about her family situation? If not, what other motives kept Nicole from telling others who might have been able to help?
7. Why do you feel that Nicole's friends never knew what was going on?
8. Has there ever been a teacher like Mrs. Rice who went out of her or his way to be helpful to you? If so, can you tell me about it?

Symbol Work

Some adolescents may be receptive to choosing a symbol for Nicole, her three friends, Mrs. Rice, and her parents, and this may be helpful to expanding the dialogue with those teens who are inhibited verbally. The choice of symbols can then be explored in each instance.

Discussion

Teens like Nicole are robbed of a carefree and protected childhood. They are thrust into adult roles and responsibilities because the parents are unable or unwilling to assume their roles as adults and/or parents. Nicole's social and activity life was constricted and stunted by the need to be at home to take care of her mom and assume responsibilities in the home that typically the parents would handle to a large extent. She was emotionally overburdened resulting in depression that she tried to hide. She was successful in masking her depression with her friends and most of her teachers with the exception of the concerned, caring, and perceptive Mrs. Rice.

There are a number of wonderful teachers, like Mrs. Rice, who are capable and caring enough to "read between the lines." These are teachers who notice when a child or teen is hurting even when young people are doing their best to hide it from everyone. Mrs. Rice to her credit did not give up. She persisted in her efforts to get to know Nicole and it paid off. An important lesson that youth like Nicole can teach us is that just as secretly they hide their pain, they also secretly want us to notice their pain.

Children and teens like Nicole have been stripped of their childhood, the only childhood they will ever have. How many young people are walking the hallways of schools everyday hiding their hurt but privately hoping that someone will notice? I don't know the answer, but it is probably more than we would ever expect. How sad, when we don't notice.

HOW THESE STRATEGIES CAN
ENHANCE THE THERAPY PROCESS

Because the emotions associated with loss—whether it is the theft of one's childhood as in Nicole's case; missing out on a secure, protective base early in life; or disrupted attachments during the ensuing years—are extremely intense, these strategies allow pre-teens and teens to approach this topic with all its attendant anxiety and threat through symbolization and metaphor.

While some older youngsters and adolescents will be able to discuss these topics directly, others will need the safety provided by the symbolism. The degree of threat that children experience in regard to these issues is evidenced by the triggering of powerful emotion when any change or shift takes place in their relational context. In residential treatment centers, it is common to observe not only violent eruptions, but runaway attempts, or even suicide attempts when another child leaves or a favorite staff member resigns, or even when a staff person goes on vacation.

Anxiety around the holidays is dramatically evident in the therapy of children who have never experienced the secure attachments and sense of a secure home that all human beings seek and need. Such was the case with Willy, a thirteen-year-old African American boy who, the night before he was to go home for Christmas to his family, became so aggressive in the dorm that it was not safe to keep him there through the night. But it is not always possible to find extra staff to come in on short notice, so after being called by the housefather at 11:00 p.m., I decided to go to the facility and take Willy to the infirmary, where I slept on one of the beds and he slept on the other. I didn't sleep well that night because I needed to be sure that Willy didn't take off and try to either run away or go back to the dorm, but he actually was relatively calm after we got him out of the dorm and down to the infirmary. I was told that once he got to sleep he usually slept soundly through the night. This is, indeed, what happened, but I nevertheless was in and out of sleep all night, checking regularly to make sure he was still there.

Since that experience, I have witnessed all too frequently the implosion of anxiety, often masked by aggressive acting-out, preceding holiday home visits. Some of the kids fear misbehaving on their visits and jeopardizing their chances of going home for good any time soon; others are worried about what they are going to find back home, particularly with parents who are or have been in the past psychiatrically ill, abusing alcohol or drugs, or prone to violence.

Willy taught me how overwhelming the anxiety can be around family holidays, and how the holidays bring to the fore intense longing and grief. The techniques in this chapter are designed for youngsters like Willy who require an indirect approach because they are too easily overwhelmed with the activation of emotions too intense for them to contain in a way that could be therapeutic. Through the safe distance provided by the stories and metaphors, the feelings and issues can be explored and examined in a supportive and empathic therapeutic context.

The Delicate Therapeutic
Operation of Facilitating Hope

*O*verview: *Creating hope is a time-honored and cherished goal of most forms of psychotherapy. It is, however, an operation that has to be approached with great sensitivity because it can have unintended side effects. Issues of timing, sensitivity, and inward monitoring of countertransference issues are critical to constructive facilitation of hope in psychotherapy with children and teens. Some strategies to explore and facilitate hope are presented and the critical issues that therapists need to monitor closely are discussed in this chapter.*

"THE BALLISTIC STALLION" (AGES 9 TO 12)

Purpose: *This story about courage and determination is told through the metaphor of a wild stallion that no one had been able to ride until Sally, the owner's twelve-year-old daughter through sheer determination and careful study of what had gone wrong in the past, finally succeeded in riding the stallion just before it was to be sold. The story then becomes a launching pad to honor the strengths and courage of children by asking the child to tell a story about a time when they triumphed over some challenge or adversity.*

"There once was a magnificent stallion that everyone admired for his strength and beauty, but no one could ride him because he bucked violently, even with the most expert and experienced riders. Often he would dump his would-be riders even before they could get settled in the saddle. One rider managed to stay on for ten seconds, but he was a champion rodeo rider who was determined and lasted ten seconds on his third try. The stallion's bucking was so wild, he became known as the "Ballistic Stallion." His owner, believing the horse would never be ridden, told his friends that he wanted to sell the horse at a reasonable price.

"Sally, his twelve-year-old daughter, was upset when she heard the news. Although she had never been allowed to try to ride the stallion, she loved watching the horse gallop in the field. She loved all horses, but she felt a special bond with the stallion because she admired his spirit. Sally was a scrappy kid herself and never liked to give up on anything that she was determined to do.

"Sally begged her dad to delay selling the horse, but he said, 'Sally, no one can ride that horse and when I get a fair price, I am going to sell him.' Sally appealed to her mother, but she said, 'Sally, your father's mind is made up; he is going to sell the Ballistic Stallion. There are other horses, and besides neither you nor anyone else can ride that stallion.' Telling Sally that she couldn't do something made her even more determined to prove that she could.

"Sally was in a race against time. She spent as much time as possible in the bottom pasture, where the stallion was fenced, studying his movements and admiring his beauty, strength, and spirit. Sally thought long and hard about all the riders who had traveled from afar to prove that they could ride the stallion when no one else could. She thought about their attitude. They had been determined to break the spirit of the stallion. In her heart she knew that this was the wrong approach.

"Sally decided to approach the challenge in a totally different way. She would not attempt, in any way, to break the spirit of the Ballistic Stallion. In fact, she would be guided by how she would want to be treated herself, since she also was high-spirited. She knew she would fight to the end if someone tried to break her spirit. She made up her mind that she would, in every way possible, honor and respect the spirit of the stallion.

"Initially, she thought she would have to race against time, but she realized that if she approached it that way, she would surely fail. She knew that to truly respect and honor the spirit of the stallion, she would have to move at his pace. Sally understood that progress might be slow with possible setbacks along the way. Perhaps her dad might sell the stallion during her efforts, but it was a chance she had to take because pressuring the stallion to go faster than he was prepared to go was doomed to failure. Fortunately, it was the beginning of the summer, giving Sally some time to put her plan in action.

"Sally's parents were aware that she loved to watch Ballistic Stallion run in the bottom ten-acre pasture, frequently bringing her binoculars to get a close-up view. They did not know, however, about her plan.

"From her position along the recently painted fence, Sally had watched Ballistic Stallion gallop numerous times. She now decided that it was time to watch the stallion from inside the fence. She climbed over and watched closely for any reaction from the stallion, but he did not seem to notice. She moved into the pasture and away from the fence about ten yards. The stallion, munching grass, looked up, but seemed unconcerned. But, immediately when Sally took another step closer, the horse took off to the far corner of the bottom pasture, running in an excited way in a large circle.

"The stallion let Sally know that she came too close. To let Ballistic Stallion know that she had understood his 'message' and that she respected the distance he needed her to keep from him, Sally not only moved back to where she was located before the horse reacted, but also clear back to the other side of the fence.

"Ballistic Stallion became curious and perhaps a little puzzled by Sally's actions. After staring in her direction for a long time, he took two more trips around the far corner of the pasture and then trotted up toward the northeast corner of the pasture where Sally was standing on the other side of the fence. To Sally's amazement, he came to a spot no more than twenty yards from where she was standing. He looked at Sally as if he were trying to size her up.

"Animals, like children, are not easily fooled. They can tell if someone really cares about them and they also know when they don't. Sally loved and admired the stallion. She felt a bond with Ballistic Stallion because they both had a strong spirit that others often just didn't understand. Their strong spirit sometimes got them both in trouble because other folks mistook their strong spirit for meanness or stubbornness. These folks just didn't understand that a strong spirited animal or person needs to be handled in a special way.

"The story of how Sally became the first person ever to ride Ballistic Stallion is a long story, but her success began when she moved to the other side of the fence when the stallion felt threatened by her nearness. The stallion learned that she respected his need to keep his distance and, as a result, he gradually came closer. He eventually allowed her to pet him, then to let her rub his nose, and, later, to give him treats of oats that he ate out of her hand. After some time, she was able to put a bridle on him and lead him around the pasture.

"There were days, however, when Ballistic Stallion would not cooperate. He did not feel comfortable, for one reason or another, and on those days, Sally made no attempt to put a bridle on him. Later on, Sally was able to put a saddle blanket on him and walk him around the field. Soon after, she was able to put on a saddle. When she first put the saddle on him, he bucked a little, but his heart was not in it.

"Ballistic Stallion knew, from the first day he sized up Sally, that she would be the first person to ride him. He knew this because he could tell that she, like him, was high-spirited and would never give up. He also knew that she understood him and would handle him according to the special way he needed.

"Sally's parents were shocked and speechless, when one late August afternoon, Sally rode the stallion right up to the front door of her house. Needless, to say, Ballistic Stallion had a home for good, and a place in Sally's heart forever."

Drawing Directives

"Now I want you to get as relaxed and comfortable as possible. If you wish, you may close your eyes. I want you to try to get a clear picture of Sally and the stallion and when you are ready, please draw them as best you can."

Follow-Up to the Drawing

1. Tell me about your drawing.
2. What title would you choose for your picture?
3. If others are included in the picture, who are they and what is the nature of the relationship with Sally and the stallion?
4. Does Sally or the Ballistic Stallion remind you of anyone?
5. If so, tell me about that person. How is that person like Sally and/or the stallion?

Storytelling Directives

"Now I would like you to think of a time when there was something you were determined to do. Perhaps, like Sally, no one thought you would be able to do it, but you did. You showed the same fighting spirit that Sally and the stallion showed. It might have been something you were afraid to do, at first, like jumping off the high diving board, but you did it. Or maybe it was a time that your parents and teachers thought you were going to fail a class, but you pulled it out. It doesn't have to be as dramatic as riding a stallion that no one else could ride, but a time when you showed the same kind of fighting spirit that Sally and the stallion showed in the story. Perhaps it was a time when you felt like giving up, but you didn't. Now, when you are ready, tell me your story."

Follow-Up to the Story

1. What would you choose for a title to your story?
2. What does the story say about your fighting spirit? Your courage? Your determination?
3. What can be learned from your story?

4. Can you think of other times when you showed the same fighting spirit and did something that no one else and perhaps even you thought you could do?
5. Pretend that you were asked to give a talk on the subject: 'Why you should never give up.' What are some of the main points you would make?

Hector's Story (age 9)   "I joined in at recess on a kickball game. Usually I would play alone because I tried many times in the past to join in but the kids would say, 'No, go away,' because I was never too good in sports. But this time I got up the courage to ask the kids to let me play. At first, they said 'No!' But then they changed their mind and I ended up having a good time. Now I play kickball almost every recess."

It is easy for adults to forget how important peer acceptance is to children and how much courage it takes for a child who has been socially rejected to risk further rejection. The story above is a good example of the kind of courage, strength, and hope that we wish to honor in children because it emanates from the exercise of resources within the child, something they can take ownership and pride in and that we, as therapists, can simply highlight and honor.

Drawing 10.1.   "The Ballistic Stallion"

Please note: Since this story presents a significant opportunity to validate strength and determination in children, the therapist can reinforce and
highlight these assets further by asking if they would like to draw a picture
showing them overcoming the odds to do something that others didn't think
could be done.

Therapeutic Use of Symbols

An alternative method is to instruct the child to pick a symbol to represent
the Ballistic Stallion, Sally, and each of her parents. In addition, the child can
be asked to pick a symbol for the courage and fighting spirit shown by the
stallion and Sally. Likewise, when the child describes their own personal tri-
umphs they can be asked to pick symbols to represent the obstacles they
faced, their courage, and a symbol for self.

Discussion

Children tend to love the story itself but more importantly it offers a natural
segue to showcasing and honoring their courage, strength, and determination
in facing difficult challenges of their own. Most children, especially with facilitation from the therapist, will be able to tell stories of times when they
overcame the odds and were victorious in facing some difficult challenge or
obstacle. This becomes an occasion to celebrate such victories and to preserve
the positive memories of such experiences to offset the experiences of defeat
and humiliation that so many of these children have experienced.

EVOCATIVE FANTASY: "THE MAGIC STONES" (AGES 6 TO 9)

Purpose: *This strategy is a modification of an evocative strategy originally created
to engage children in meaningful dialogue around the three critical domains in their
interpersonal world—family, school, and friends—and concludes with a focus on
their relationship to self (Crenshaw, 2006b). Younger children are fascinated with
magic and mystery. It is modified here for the purpose of exploring the children's fan-
tasies about the lives, if they could magically choose, they would like for themselves
in the past, present, and future.*

Directives

"I want you to pretend that you visit an interesting gift shop and you notice
three small, beautifully designed wooden boxes. You decide to open the

three boxes and find each contains a magic stone. In the first box, underneath the stone is a note that says, 'When you hold this magic stone in your hand, you can change anything you wish about your past life.' In the second box under the magic stone the note states, 'When held in your hand this magic stone permits you to change anything you wish about your present life.' In the third box under the magic stone is a note that says, 'This magic stone when held in your hand makes it possible for you to create the life you would want for yourself in the future.' Now let's start with magic stone that you hold in your hand that allows you to change anything you want about your life in the past."

Note to therapists: The stones I use are quite colorful and beautiful and were purchased in various gift shops and are readily available. If the therapist does not have a collection of stones, fancy buttons of different designs and shapes will do fine. To add to the suspense and drama for the kids I enclose each of the stones in a Vyatka straw-inlaid box. These beautiful and unique boxes come from the city of Vyatka, in the Kirov area of Central Russia. This traditional folk art item is now available outside of Russia. These strikingly pretty Vyatka straw boxes are handmade of European linden or birch. Then the straw is cut into small pieces, dried, and hand-glued or inlaid to make the intricate geometric designs. The last step is to lacquer the box to fix the design. Children are fascinated with the beauty of both the stones and the boxes that contain them and it lends an air of distinction and importance to this fantasy strategy.

Follow-Up Sample Questions

1. What would you want to change about your past life if you had magical powers?
2. What would you like to change about your present life?
3. What kind of life would you want to create for yourself in the future?
4. What things in your present life would you like to keep just the way they are and see them continue into the future?
5. Although we can't change our past, we can learn from it. Are there some valuable lessons that you have learned from the things that went wrong in your past?
6. We can make changes in the present. Can you think of some changes that you would like to make to your life in the present?
7. We can also take small steps toward creating the future we would like. Can you think of some small steps you can take toward the life you would like to have in the future?

"THE TREE ON TOP OF THE HILL"
(STRATEGY FOR AGES 7 TO 12)

Purpose: *This story more than the others in this book allows for considerable lee-way in the child's story since there is considerable ambiguity and many possible sto-ries the child can tell when assuming the voice of the tree that has seen many things and endured adversity and hardship during the hundreds of years of its existence. It should be remembered, however, that while such ambiguity allows children to pro-ject their inner life into the story of the tree, we cannot always assume this to be the case. It simply may be that a creative child tells an extremely imaginative story about a tree. As Freud reminded us, sometimes a cigar is just a cigar.*

The Story

"A long time ago, in a far away land, a tree was planted on the top of a hill overlooking a castle occupied by a king. The castle has long since decayed and fallen into ruin. The walls crumbled; weeds grew in what used to be the courtyard. The dungeon that many centuries ago held prisoners who dis-obeyed the decrees of the king long ago collapsed and was covered by rocks. There have been many changes in the land since the tree was planted, and kings and queens no longer rule the country. Over the tree's life there were numerous battles and wars, and also famine, droughts, and sickness. But the tall, proud tree at the top of the hill still stands. It truly is a strong tree with great dignity."

Drawing Directives

"Now, try to picture that tree standing tall and proud on top of the hill. When you are ready, please draw as best you can that tree on top of the hill. Draw the tree that has survived and weathered so many hard times, but still stands tall and proud."

Follow-Up to the Drawing

1. What title could you give to your drawing?
2. If the tree could feel what would it be feeling in your picture?
3. What is the relationship of any others in the picture to the tree?
4. Is the tree in your picture healthy or sick?
5. Is it strong or weak?
6. How long will the tree in your drawing live?
7. Who cares about the tree?

Storytelling Directives

"Every person who has been on a long journey has many interesting stories to tell. This tree has had a long journey and has lived through many changes. If the tree could talk what stories would it tell? The tree has seen and survived so many challenges. The people of the village knew it had many stories it could tell. Pretend that the people who live in the village climbed the steep hill and are gathered around to hear the story of the tree." The child then becomes the voice of the tree and tells one of its many stories to the villagers.

Follow-Up to the Story

Therapists can look for central and emotionally significant themes that capture key feelings or conflicts with which the child is struggling and then cross-validate these themes by examining the child's other stories. The therapist can then employ metaphors that will capture, in a powerful way, these central themes, feelings, and conflicts. The themes can also be used in interpretative activity and in reflections upon subsequent artistic creations. Some additional questions that might be asked of the child follow:

1. What made the tree decide to tell its story?
2. Why did he pick this time to do it?
3. What would be a good title for the tree's story?
4. What did the village people learn from the tree's story?
5. Does that tall, strong, proud tree that has survived so much remind you of anyone?

Jose's Story (age 9) "The wars were awful, how bloody the hill was that he was on and how many scars he had. How nice it was during the winter, spring, summer, and fall. He told the people of the village how people's houses had changed over the past few hundred years. They were first built out of logs, stone, and brick. Now houses are built with all kinds of modern materials. People were short and tall and now they are more normal size. People used to be gruesome, now they are nicer. He tells them a ghost story. People like them, now they have nightmares; they are really good ghost stories."

This story is very typical of children who have been exposed to either violence or trauma. "People used to be gruesome," but now reflecting his more stable life in an adoptive home, "Now they are nicer." He still has nightmares, but they are not as frightening and chilling as before: "People like them; they are really good ghost stories." I have found the tree to be a symbol of life and its endurance through hard times pulls for the adversities that many children, especially those resistant to talk therapy, have experienced, weathered, and

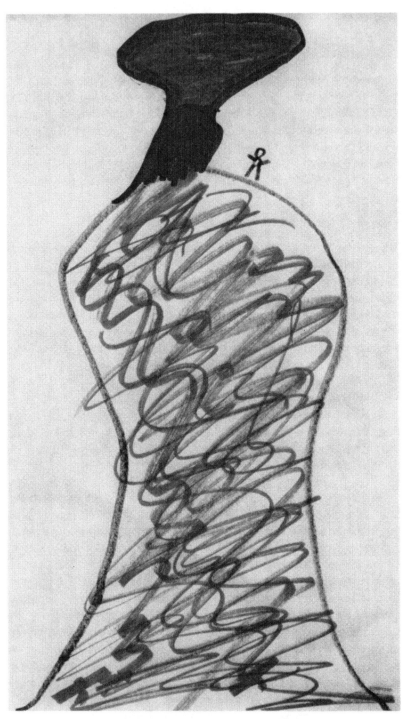

Drawing 10.2. "The Tree on Top of the Hill"

survived. The tree can become a symbol of resilience in children marking their ability to make it through difficult times. Through the tree, the children can begin to tell their life story, although typically in small segments at a time. This is healthy. After all, if a child spilled everything in response to a single drawing or story, I would worry about the child's lack of defenses.

Symbol Work with "The Tree on Top of the Hill"

Some children may benefit from selecting a tree from a collection of minia-tures and placing it on a mound created in a sand box or using blocks to cre-ate an elevated platform and then selecting miniatures to represent the vil-lagers gathered to hear the stories of the tree. Informed particularly by the work of Violet Oaklander (1988) and Eliana Gil (2006), the child can be in-vited to be the voice of the tree. The villagers, who are given their voices by the therapist, can ask a series of questions to understand the stories of the tree better. Some examples of typical questions that can be asked by the villagers are shown below:

1. Are there other stories you would like to tell us?
2. What is your favorite story to tell?
3. How have you survived all the hard seasons you have been through?
4. What was the hardest period you have faced so far?
5. What was the most valuable lesson you have learned?
6. Do you have any advice you would like to give to the villagers?
7. Do you ever get lonely?
8. Do you have any friends among the animals who visit you?
9. How did you become so strong?
10. How do you feel when you lose your leaves in the fall?

When remaining in the metaphor as illustrated above, it is important not to overinterpret the child's responses. While it is assumed that through the symbol of the tree, the children are telling their own stories about their own lives, we should not read too much into one story. Rather we should look for patterns and common themes over time and across stories that weave a con-sistent narrative that we may more confidently assume reflects important as-pects of their inner feelings pertaining to their experiences.

Discussion

Hope, Courage, Strength, and Resilience   The courage of children, their strength, resilience, and determination to persevere in the face of severe obstacles is inspiring. I marvel at their ability to learn to trust again, their willingness to forgive, their ability, at times, to still smile and laugh, when there is so much pain in their lives. I treasure their ability to dream new dreams, to retain their sense of wonder, and to maintain their fighting spirit. As adults, however, we can't afford to delude ourselves into believing that children, no matter what their environment, will somehow be resilient and turn out okay. Some environments are so toxic that sadly, the children can't recover.

Garbarino (1999) makes this point when he discussed research on inner city youth in Chicago growing up in poor and high-crime neighborhoods (Tolan and Guerra, 1994). The findings suggest that no matter how resilient a child may be, when social conditions are poisonous to an extreme degree the adverse impact can overwhelm whatever resources exist in the child and family to achieve a better life.

Crucial to working with children who were exposed to horrific things is a therapeutic attitude of healthy respect for the child's defenses and how they protect the child from further harm. It would be the height of therapeutic narcissism to expect that because we are "warm and fuzzy," the child should drop their defenses, give up their guardedness, and open up to us. We should be glad they have these defenses. Even though their defenses may be primitive, they enable such children to survive in the face of difficult obstacles.

Some, in their short lives, have experienced and survived more horror than their adult therapist has encountered in a significantly longer life. The children can teach us about survival, resilience, toughness, and perseverance in the face of extreme hardships and adversity. Our goal is not to get them to shed their primitive defenses, but rather to use them in a more conscious, deliberate, and flexible way until they can develop more mature ones.

Therapists should always reframe defenses as adaptive and honor and respect them. Paradoxically, when the therapist approaches therapy with this attitude, the child will have less need for their defenses because the therapy has become a safe place (Havens, 1989). Most parents mean well and do not deliberately subject their children to toxic and poisonous emotional climates. Nevertheless, I never cease to be amazed by how the imminent threat of rupture in human attachments can bring out the worst in people. At such times, parents, who ordinarily are quite concerned about their children's welfare, can engage in parental warfare that has a nuclear fallout for their children and the results can be tragic.

The "tree that has seen so much, and weathered many hard times," often represents for children a powerful symbol of a "survivor" who has faced difficult conditions and perhaps witnessed painful things, but stands "tall and proud" on top of the hill. This story can symbolize hope, survival, and strength, while validating the difficult life that many survivors have endured.

It avoids the problem of minimizing the adversities that youth have surmounted in order to reach a place of more hopeful possibilities.

Why Is Creating Hope a Delicate Operation?

The therapeutic process of creating hope while a valued goal of most approaches is nevertheless a most delicate operation. Walter Bonime told me in psychoanalytic supervision that hope could be dangerous. At first, I could not comprehend that notion. With greater clinical experience I began to appreciate what Dr. Bonime meant. It was driven home to me in a dramatic way when a young teen client of mine made a serious suicide attempt after a breakthrough that was extremely hopeful and uplifting to both of us. Some people survive by keeping expectations low. This is sometimes called a "survival orientation" (Hardy and Laszloffy, 2005) or "terminal thinking" (Garbarino, 1995, 1999). If your dreams and hopes have been crushed repeatedly, to entertain hope is dangerous. As therapists we must be sensitive to this issue. Children and families may feel that their very survival depends on keeping expectations low and not daring to hope for too much or to look too far into the future. Their orientation may be one of, "How can I survive another day?"

This issue of creating hope can also be complicated by countertransference feelings as well. The therapist may have a need to move their youthful or family clients to a better, more hopeful place before it makes sense to those children and their families. The need belongs to the therapist not the clients. The countertransference issue may derive from the need to prove adequacy by attempting to move clients before they are ready to a more hopeful outlook or it may be driven by the need of the therapist to flee the dark place of despair and hopelessness that the clients currently occupy. This would be true of "affect phobic" therapists (Hardy, personal communication, August, 2004) who are unable to join with clients when they are in a space of profound rage or sorrow.

Whatever the driving force, because it is not in keeping with the true needs of the clients, the therapist's actions would be considered not only antitherapeutic but even worse—they risk insulting the child or family because it leaves the impression that their pain is being trivialized or not taken seriously. Children and families, like all human beings, need hope but in the therapeutic endeavor it must be facilitated in a careful and sensitive manner, with thoughtful consideration of the emotional place that the clients currently occupy, with utmost skill and timing, for indeed this is one of our most risky interventions, particularly if we don't understand and are insensitive to these considerations.

HOW THESE STRATEGIES CAN
ENHANCE THE THERAPY PROCESS

The Ballistic Stallion and *The Tree on Top of the Hill* avoid some of the therapeutic pitfalls described in the previous section. Rather than offering empty reassurance, *The Ballistic Stallion* is used as a springboard to focus on strengths located in the children. The children tell a story about a time when they did something courageous or difficult that perhaps no one thought they could do. Instead of relying on the optimism of the therapist or the strengths of the therapist, the children base their hope on their own resources located within them and not dependent on the continuance of the therapy or the presence of the therapist.

The Magic Stones technique offers a playful opportunity for the young child to consider their past, present life, and the life they would like to have in the future. While the past can't be changed, there may be important lessons to learn from the past that can be used in the present or to build toward a better future. By focusing on what is possible to change in the present and what small steps can be taken toward the life they wish for in the future, the therapist is laying a foundation for hope that is realistic and based on what is important to the child. Even though the exercise is couched in terms of "magical stones" there is nothing magical about the learning from the past, making changes in the present, and taking small steps toward a better future. The magical, fanciful exercise simply creates a portal of entry that makes it less threatening for the child to examine the lessons of the past, and to consider changes in the present, and steps to take for the future.

The Tree on Top of the Hill in metaphor honors the trials and suffering of the survivors as well as their strengths in weathering adverse conditions but in the end "still standing tall and proud on top of the hill." This avoids the hazard that child clients might view the therapist as taking their struggles lightly because the tree has survived many harsh winters, and faced adversities of all kinds but nevertheless survives and remains strong. This story creates hope as well as validates the suffering of the survivor. This is the delicate balance that must be achieved if we are to facilitate hope in survivors whose hopes and dreams have been crushed all too often. It is the delicate, well-timed and paced, and skillful work of empathic healing.

RESOURCES FOR CLINICIANS
REFERRED TO IN THIS CHAPTER

The Vyatka straw boxes can be ordered from the Russian American Company, (800) 742-6228, www.russianamericancompany.com.

References

Algom, D., Chajut, E, and Lev, S. (2004). A rational look at the emotional Stroops phenomenon: A generic slowdown, not a Stroop effect. *Journal of Experimental Psychology: General, 133*, 323–38.

Allison, S., Stacey, K., Dadds, V., Roeger, L., Wood, A., and Martin, G. (2003). What the family brings: Gathering evidence for strengths-based work. *Journal of Family Therapy, 25*, 263–284.

Ammons, R. B., and Ammons, C. H. (1980). Use and evaluation of the Kahn Test of Symbol Arrangement (KTSA): Partial summary through October, 1979. I: Published papers. *Perceptual and Motor Skills, 50*, 127–130.

Anderson, A. K. (2005). Affective influences on the attentional dynamics supporting awareness. *Journal of Experimental Psychology: General, 134*, 258–281.

Bina, M., Graziano, F., and Bonino, S. (2006). Risky driving and lifestyles in adolescence. *Accident Analysis & Prevention, 38*, 472–481.

Bonime, W. (1962). *The clinical use of dreams.* New York: Basic Books.

Bonime, W. (1989). *Collaborative psychoanalysis: Anxiety, depression, dreams, and personality change.* Rutherford, N.J.: Fairleigh Dickinson Press.

Bowlby, J. (1980). *Attachment and loss.* New York: Basic Books.

Boyd, J., and Ross, K. (1994). The courage tapes: A positive approach to life's challenges. *Journal of Systemic Therapies, 13*, 64–69.

Bromberg, P. (1998). *Standing in the spaces: Essays on clinical process, trauma, and dissociation.* Hillsdale, N.J.: Analytic Press.

Brooks, R. (1993). *The search for islands of competence.* Presentation at the Fifth Annual Conference of CHADD. San Diego, Calif.

Brooks, R. (2003). *Facilitating hope and resilience in children.* Keynote presentation at the Fiftieth Anniversary Conference of the Astor Home for Children. Fishkill, N.Y.

Burke, A. E., Crenshaw, D. A., Green, J., Schlosser, M. A., and Rivera, L. S. (1989). Influence of verbal ability on the expression of aggression in physically abused children. *Journal of the American Academy of Child and Adolescent Psychiatry, 28,* 215–218.

Carey, L. (1998). *Sand play therapy with children and families.* Northvale, N.J.: Jason Aronson.

Carey, L., (Ed.) (2006). *Expressive and creative arts methods for trauma survivors.* London: Jessica Kingsley Publishers.

Church, E. (1994). The role of autonomy in adolescent psychotherapy. *Psychotherapy: Theory, Research, Practice, Training, 31,* 101–108.

Clark, M. D. (1998). Strengths-based practice: The ABC's of working with adolescents who don't want to work with you. *Federal Probation, 62,* 46–53.

Cooper, J. C. (1978). *An illustrated encyclopaedia of traditional symbols.* London: Thames and Hudson.

Corcoran, J. (1997). A solution-oriented approach to working with juvenile offenders. *Child and Adolescent Social Work Journal, 14,* 277–88.

Corcoran, J. (2005). *Building strengths and skills: A collaborative approach to working with clients.* New York: Oxford University Press.

Craddick, R. A., and L'Abate, L. (1972). The Kahn Test of Symbol Arrangement (KTSA): A second critical review. *International Journal of Symbology, 1*(Mono.): 1–33.

Crenshaw, D. A. (1995). The crisis of connection: Children of multiple loss and trauma. *Grief Work, 1,* 16–21.

Crenshaw, D. A. (2004). *Engaging resistant children in therapy: Projective drawing and storytelling strategies.* Rhinebeck, N.Y.: Rhinebeck Child and Family Center Publications.

Crenshaw, D. A. (2005). Clinical tools to facilitate treatment of childhood traumatic grief. *Omega: Journal of Death and Dying, 51,* 239–255.

Crenshaw, D. A. (2006a). Neuroscience and trauma treatment: Implications for creative art therapists. In L. C. Carey (Ed.), *Expressive and creative arts methods for trauma survivors, (*pp. 1–25). London: Jessica Kingsley Publishers.

Crenshaw, D. A. (2006b). *Evocative strategies in child and adolescent psychotherapy.* Lanham, Md.: Jason Aronson/Rowman & Littlefield Publishing.

Crenshaw, D. A. (2006c). *The Heartfelt Feelings Strategy.* Rhinebeck, N.Y.: Rhinebeck Child and Family Center Publications.

Crenshaw, D. A. (2007a). *The Heartfelt Feelings Coloring Cards Strategies Manual.* Rhinebeck, N.Y.: Rhinebeck Child and Family Center Publications.

Crenshaw, D. A. (2007b). An interpersonal neurobiological-informed treatment model for childhood traumatic grief. *Omega, 54,* 315–332.

Crenshaw, D. A. (in press a). *The Symbol Association Therapy Strategies (SATS) Clinical Manual.* Rhinebeck, NY: Rhinebeck Child and Family Center Publications.

Crenshaw, D. A. (in press a). *Supervision of play therapists in working with aggressive children.* In A. Drewes and J. Mullen (Eds.), *Supervision can be playful: Play techniques for child and play therapists.* Lanham, Md.: Jason Aronson/Rowman & Littlefield.

Crenshaw, D. A., and Garbarino, J. (2007). The hidden dimensions: Profound sorrow and buried human potential in violent youth. *Journal of Humanistic Psychology, 47,* 160–174.

Crenshaw, D. A., and Hardy, K. V. (2005). Understanding and treating the aggression of traumatized children in out-of-home care. In N. Boyd-Webb, (Ed.), *Working with traumatized youth in child welfare,* (pp. 171–195). New York: Guilford.

Crenshaw, D. A., and Hardy, K. V. (in press). The crucial role of empathy in breaking the silence of traumatized children in play therapy. *International Journal of Play Therapy.*

Crenshaw, D. A., and Mordock, J. B. (2005a) *A handbook of play therapy with aggressive children.* Lanham, Md.: Jason Aronson/Rowman & Littlefield Publishing.

Crenshaw, D. A., and Mordock, J. B. (2005b). *Understanding and treating the aggression of children: Fawns in gorilla suits.* Lanham, Md.: Jason Aronson/Rowman & Littlefield Publishing.

Darwin, J. (2007). Hidden language: Hidden agendas. *PsycCRITIQUES, 52,* Release 33, Article 175.

DeDomenico, G. (1999). Group sand tray-worldplay: New dimensions in sandplay therapy. In D. Sweeney and L. Homeyer (Eds.), *The handbook of group play therapy: How to do it, how it works, whom it's best for,* (pp. 215–33). San Francisco: Jossey-Bass Publishers.

DeYoung, P. (2003). *Relational psychotherapy: A primer.* New York: Brunner-Routledge.

Drewes, A. (2001). The Gingerbread Person Feelings Map. In H.G. Kaduson and C. E. Schaefer (Eds.), *101 more favorite play therapy techniques,* (pp. 92–97). Northvale, N.J.: Jason Aronson.

Drobes, D. J., Elibero, A.. and Evans, D. E. (2006). Attentional bias for smoking and affective stimuli: A Stroop Task Study. *Psychology of Addictive Behaviors, 20,* 490–495.

Epley, N., Savitsky, K., and Gilovich, T. (2002). Empathy neglect: Reconciling the spotlight effect and the correspondence bias. *Journal of Personality & Social Psychology, 83,* 300–312.

Erskine, R. G. (2001). The psychotherapist's myths, dreams, and realities. *International Journal of Psychotherapy, 6,* 133–140.

Fraiberg, S., Adelson, E.. and Shapiro, V. (1965). Ghosts in the nursery. *Journal of the American Academy of Child Psychiatry, 14,* 387–424.

Fulkerson, J. A., Story, M., Mellin, A., Leffert, N., Neumark-Sztainer, D., and French, S. A. (2006). Family dinner meal frequency and adolescent development: Relationships with developmental assets and high-risk behaviors. *Journal of Adolescent Health, 39,* 337–345

Furth, G. M. (2002). *The secret world of drawings: A Jungian approach to healing through art.* Toronto: Inner City Books.

Garaigordobil, M., and de Galdeano, P. G. (2006). Empatía en niños de 10 a 12 años. / Empathy in children aged 10 to 12 years. *Psicothema, 18,* 180–186.

Garbarino, J. (1995). *Raising children in a socially toxic environment.* San Francisco: Jossey-Bass.

Garbarino, J. (1999). *Lost boys: Why our sons turn violent and how we can save them.* New York: Anchor Books.

Garbarino, J. (March, 22, 2006). *Words can hurt forever.* Daniel Kirk Memorial Lecture at Marist College, Poughkeepsie, N.Y.

Garbarino, J., and Crenshaw, D. A. (in press). Seeking a shelter for the soul. In D. A. Crenshaw (Ed.), *Child and Adolescent Psychotherapy: Wounded Spirits and Healing Paths*. Lanham, Md.: Jason Aronson/Rowman & Littlefield Publishing.

Gil, E. (1991). *The healing power of play*. New York: Guilford.

Gil, E. (2006). *Helping abused and traumatized children: Integrating directive and nondirective approaches*. New York: Guilford Press.

Gil, E., and L. Rubin. (2005). Countertransference play: Informing and enhancing therapist self-awareness through play. *International Journal of Play Therapy, 14,* 87–102.

Goodyear-Brown, P. (2002). *Digging for buried treasure*. Antioch, Tenn.: Paris Goodyear Brown.

Gruhn, D., Smith, J., and Baltes, P. B. (2005). No aging bias favoring memory for positive material: Evidence from a heterogeneity-homogeneity list paradigm using emotionally toned words. *Psychology and Aging, 20,* 579–588.

Hadley, C. B., and MacKay, D. G. (2006). Does emotion help or hinder immediate memory? Arousal versus priority-binding mechanisms. *Journal of Experimental Psychology: Learning, Memory, and Cognition, 32,* 79–88.

Hanna, F. J., and Hunt, W. P. (1999). Techniques for psychotherapy with defiant, aggressive adolescents. *Psychotherapy: Theory, Research, Practice, Training, 36,* 56–68.

Hardy, K. V. (2000). *Psychological homelessness*. Presentation at the Family Therapy Networker Symposium. Washington, D.C.

Hardy, K. V. (2003). *Working with aggressive and violent youth*. Presentation at the Psychotherapy Networker Symposium. Washington, DC.

Hardy, K. V., and Crenshaw D. A. (in press) Healing Wounds to the soul camouflaged by rage. In D. A. Chenshaw (Ed.) Child and Adolescent Psychotherapy: Wounded Spirits and Healing Paths. Lanham, MD: Jason Aronson/Rowman & Littlefield.

Hardy, K. V., and Laszloffy, T. A. (2005). *Teens who hurt: Clinical interventions to break the cycle of adolescent violence.* New York: Guilford.

Hastings, P. D., Zahn-Waxler, C., Robinson, J., Usher, B., and Bridges, D. (2000). The development of concern for others in children with behavior problems. *Developmental Psychology, 36,* 531–546.

Havens, L. (1989). A safe place. Cambride, MA: Harvard University Press.

Horvath, A. O. (2001). The alliance. *Psychotherapy: Theory, Research, Practice, Training, 38,* 365–372.

Helton, L. R., and Smith, M. K. (2004). *Mental health practice with children and youth: A strengths and well-being model.* New York: The Haworth Press.

James, B. (1989). *Treating traumatized children: New insights and creative interventions.* Lexington, Mass: Lexington Books.

Johnson, N. G. (2003). On treating adolescent girls: Focus on strengths and resiliency in psychotherapy. *Journal of Clinical Psychology, 59,* 1193–1203.

Jung, C. G. (1961). *Memories, dreams, reflections*. New York: Random House.

Kahn, T. C. (1951). An original test of symbol arrangement validated on organic psychotics. *Journal of Consulting Psychology 15,* 439–444.

Kahn, T. C. (1957). *The Kahn Test of Symbol Arrangement*. Psychological Tests Specialists.

Kahn, T. C., and Murphy, P. D. (1958). A new symbol approach to personality assessment. *American Journal of Psychiatry, 114,* 741–743.

Kalff, D. M. (1971). *Sandplay: A mirror of the psyche.* San Francisco: Browser Press.

Kalff, D. M. (1980). *Sandplay: A psychotherapeutic approach to the psyche.* Boston: Siglo Press.

Kazdin, A. E. (2005). Treatment outcomes, common factors, and continued neglect of mechanisms of change. *Clinical Psychology: Science and Practice, 12,* 184–88.

Klorer, P. G. (2000). *Expressive therapy with troubled children.* Northvale, NJ: Jason Aronson.

Kopp, S. (1970). The Wizard of Oz behind the couch. *Psychology Today, 3,* 70–73, 84.

L'Abate, L., and Craddick., R. A. (1965). The Kahn Test of Symbol Arrangement (KTSA): A critical review. *Journal of Clinical Psychology, 21,* 115–35.

Land, J. C. (2000). *Fun with feelings workbook. Volume I.* Louisville, Ky.: Jane C. Land.

Lawrence, E., (2003) A competence-based approach to family therapy. Presentation at the Astor Home 50th Anniversary Conference Fiskin, NY.

LeBel, J., Stromberg, N., Duckworth, K., Kerzner, J., Goldstein, M., and Weeks, G., et al. (2004). Child and adolescent inpatient restraint reduction: A state initiative to promote strength-based care. *Journal of the American Academy of Child & Adolescent Psychiatry, 43,* 37–45.

Levine, M. D. (2002) *A mind at a time.* New York: Touchstone Books.

Liddle, H. A. (1995). Conceptual and clinical dimensions of multidimensional, multisystems engagement strategy in family-based adolescent treatment. *Psychotherapy, 32,* 39–58.

Lietz, C. A. (2004). Resiliency based social learning: Strengths based approach to residential treatment. *Residential Treatment for Children & Youth, 22,* 21–36.

Loar, L. (2001). Eliciting cooperation from teenagers and their parents. *Journal of Systemic Therapies, 20,* 59–77.

Lowenfeld, M. (1939). The World pictures of children: A method of recording and studying them. *British Journal of Medical Psychology 18,* 65–101.

Lowenfeld, M. (1979). *The World Technique.* London: George Allen and Unwin.

Lowenstein, L. (2006). *Creative interventions for bereaved children.* Toronto: Champion Press.

Magnavita, Jeffrey J. (2006). In search of the unifying principles of psychotherapy: Conceptual, empirical, and clinical convergence: *American Psychologist, 61,* 882–892.

Malchiodi, C. (2003). (Ed.). *Handbook of art therapy.* New York: Guilford Press.

Malchiodi, C. A. (1998). *Understanding children's drawings.* New York: Guilford.

May, R. (1975). Values, myths, and symbols. *American Journal of Psychiatry, 132,* 703–706.

McMahon, S., Wernsman, J., and Parnes, A. (2006). Understanding prosocial behavior: The impact of empathy and gender among African American adolescents. *Journal of Adolescent Health, 39,* 135–137.

Miller, J. B. (1986). *What do we mean by relationships?* Wellesley, Mass.: Stone Center for Developmental Services and Studies.

Miller, J. B., and Stiver, I. P. (1997). *The healing connection: How women form relationships in therapy and life.* Boston: Beacon Press.

Minuchin, S., and Colapinto, J. (October, 1994). Consultation to the Astor Home for Children, Rhinebeck, N.Y.

Minuchin, S., and Fishman, H. C. (1981). *Family therapy techniques.* Cambridge, Mass.: Harvard University Press.

Minuchin, S., and Nichols, M. P. (1993). *Family healing: Tales of hope and renewal from family therapy.* New York: The Free Press.

Mitchell, S. A. (Ed), and Aaron, L. (Ed). (1999). *Relational psychoanalysis: The emergence of a tradition.* Relational Perspectives Book Series, Vol. 14. Mahwah, N.J.: Analytic Press.

Nickerson, A. B., Salamone, F. J., Brooks, J. L., and Colby, S. A. (2004). Promising approaches to engaging families and building strengths in residential treatment. *Residential Treatment for Children & Youth, 22,* 1–18.

Norcross, J. C. (2001). Purposes, processes, and products of the task force on empirically supported therapy relationships. *Psychotherapy: Theory, Research, Practice, Training, 38,* 345–356.

Oaklander, V. (1988). *Windows to our children.* Highland, N.Y.: The Center for Gestalt Development.

O'Connor, K. (1983). The Color-Your-Life Technique. In C. Schaefer and K. O'Connor (Eds.), *The handbook of play therapy,* (pp. 251–257). New York: John Wiley.

O'Donohue, J. (1997). *The invisible world.* (An audio recording) Louisville, Colo.: Sounds True, Inc.

Oetzel, K. B., and Scherer, D. G. (2003). Therapeutic engagement with adolescents in psychotherapy. *Psychotherapy: Theory, Research, Practice, Training, 40,* 215–225.

O'Sullivan, J. (2005). It's 420: Do you know where your children are? Adolescent substance use and misuse. *Clinical Excellence for Nurse Practitioners, 9,* 127–29.

Pepi, C. L. (1997). Children without childhoods: A feminist intervention strategy utilizing systems theory and restorative justice in treating female adolescent offenders. *Women & Therapy 20,* 85–101.

Querimit, D. S., and Conner, L. C. (2003). Empowerment psychotherapy with adolescent females of color. *Journal of Clinical Psychology, 59,* 1215–1224.

Reyna, V. F., and Farley, F. (2006). Risk and rationality in adolescent decision making: Implications for theory, practice, and public policy. *Psychological Science in the Public Interest, 7,* 1–44.

Riviere, S. (2005). Play therapy to engage adolescents. In L. Gallo-Lopez and C. E. Schaefer (Eds.) *Play therapy with adolescents,* 2nd ed. (pp. 121–142). Lanham, Md.: Jason Aronson/Rowman & Littlefield.

Rourke, B. P. (Ed). (1995). *Syndrome of nonverbal learning disabilities: Neurodevelopmental manifestations.* New York: Guilford.

Rubenstein, A. K. (1996). Interventions for a scattered generation: Treating adolescents in the nineties. *Psychotherapy: Theory, Research, Practice, Training, 33,* 353–360.

Sarnoff, C. A. (1987). *Psychotherapeutic strategies in the latency years.* Northvale, N.J.: Jason Aronson, Inc.

Schore, A. N. (1994). *Affect regulation and the origin of the self: The neurobiology of emotional development.* Hillsdale, N.J.: Erlbaum.

Schore, A. N. (2003a). *Affect dysregulation and disorders of the self.* New York: Norton.
Schore, A. N. (2003b). *Affect regulation and the repair of the self.* New York: Norton.
Siegel, D. (1999). *The developing mind: How relationships and the brain interact to shape who we are.* New York: Guilford.
Siegel, D. (2007). *The mindful brain: Reflections and attunement in the cultivation of well-being.* New York: Norton.
Silverstein, O. (1987). *The art of systems therapy.* A presentation at the Ackerman Institute for the Family. New York, N.Y.
Tangney, J. P., and Dearing, R. L. (2002). *Shame and guilt.* New York: Guilford Press.
Van der Kolk, B. (2003). The neurobiology of childhood trauma and abuse. *Child and Adolescent Psychiatric Clinics of North America, 12,* 293–317.
Volkan, V. D. (1981). *Linking objects and linking phenomenon.* New York: International Universities Press.
Volkan, V. D. (1999). Nostalgia as a linking phenomenon. *Journal of Applied Psychoanalytic Studies, 1,* 169–179.
Waters, D. B., and Lawrence, E. (1993). *Competence, courage and change: An approach to family therapy.* New York: Norton.
White, R. (1959). Motivation reconsidered: The concept of competence. *Psychological Review* 66: 297–333.
Worden, J. W. (1996). *Children and grief: When a parent dies.* New York: Guilford Press.
Williams, K. D. (2007). Ostracism. *Annual Review of Psychology, 58,* 425–452.
Zahn-Waxler, C., Park, J.-H., Essex, M., Slattery, M., and Cole, P. M. (2005). Relational and overt aggression in disruptive adolescents: Prediction from early social representations and links with concurrent problems. *Early Education and Development, 16,* 259–282.
Zahn-Waxler, C., Usher, B., Suomi, S., and Cole, P. M. (2005). Intersections of biology and behavior in young children's antisocial patterns: The role of development, gender and socialization. In D. M. Stoff and E. J. Susman, (Eds). *Developmental psychobiology of aggression,* (pp. 141–160). New York, N.Y.: Cambridge University Press.

Index

abuse, 72, 75, 108, 135
ADHD, 64, 92, 129
affect regulation, 7, 9
aggression, 64, 74, 88, 93, 99
alliance, therapeutic, 2–6, 45–55, 22–23,
   27, 73, 128–29
anxiety, 5, 26, 65–66, 83, 124, 132, 141,
   143–44
attachment theory, 6, 8, 10, 12, 17,
   22–5, 71, 118–19, 132, 143, 156
attachments, key, 17, 22–23, 25
art therapy, 3–4, 8–9

Bonime, W., 3, 8, 11, 30, 41–42, 65, 157
Bowlby, J., 2, 131
Brooks, R., 53–54

Carey, L., 30
cautions, clinical, 4–6, 76
compassion, 10, 58–59, 91, 93
contraindications, 5, 126
coping, 5, 49, 51, 57, 99, 137
countertransference, 6, 15–16, 26, 30,
   40, 145, 157
courage: stories of courage, 24, 45–6,
   51–52, 70, 102, 104, 145; courage in
   children, 49–52, 55, 148–50, 155,
   158; courage in families, 54; courage,
   references, 165

Dearing, R. L., 60, 96
DeDomenico, G. 30
defenses, 22, 76, 105, 132, 155–56
depression, 26, 38, 49, 69, 81, 87, 99,
   141, 143
determination, 24, 45–46, 49–52, 145,
   148, 150
drawings: drawings as a therapy tool,
   2–4, 6, 10, 18, 22, 25,-26, 36–37, 50;
   specific drawing techniques, 46,
   52–53, 59–71, 78, 80, 88, 90–91,
   101–03, 106   109, 112–14, 120,
   122–25; 130, 135, 137, 141, 148–49,
   152, 154–55 ; drawings, references,
   160, 162, 164
dreams, 30, 41–42, 74, 132, 137–39,
   156–58

empathy, 3, 6, 29, 64, 83–97, 114–115
expressive domains, 9, 12, 17–22, 27–29,
   35

family systems theory, 2, 15, 124
family therapy, 6, 15–16, 26, 30, 34, 54
fear, 1, 15, 19, 49, 66–67, 71, 77, 86,
   123–24, 144
foster care, 25, 71, 123, 132
Fraiberg, S., 93, 161
Furth, G., 4, 162

Garbarino, J., 74–75, 93, 108, 131–32, 156–57
Gil, E., 8, 10, 16, 30, 86, 155
grief , 19, 117–30, 144
group therapy, 3, 8, 15
guilt, 19, 60, 80, 96, 165

Hardy, K., 54, 61, 74–75, 93, 108, 125, 132, 157
healing, 3–4, 6, 16, 27, 62, 86, 93, 97, 126–28, 158
high-risk behaviors, adolescents, 75–76, 80–82
hope: hope as a therapeutic ingredient 2, 6, 19, 49, 53–55, 60, 64, 72, 74, 97, 105, 113–114 ; specific strategies regarding hope,137–39 145–58; hope, reference, 164

identity, 47, 74
intimacy, 123–24

James, B., 8
Jung, C., 29–30, 41

Kahn, T., 30–32
Kalff, D. M., 30
Klorer, P. G., 4
Kopp, S., 65

Laszloffy, T., 54, 74, 93, 108, 125, 157
longing, 37, 40, 124, 131–32, 144
loss, 25, 37, 52, 71–72, 74, 80, 117, 119, 124–26, 130, 132–33, 143
love, 9–10, 16, 19, 21, 24–25, 31, 37, 51, 60, 108, 121, 127–28, 129–30, 146–47
Lowenfeld, M., 30

Malchiodi, C., 4, 22
meaning, 12, 30, 40–42, 57, 62–63, 68, 82, 90, 118, 131
Miller, J. B., 2, 54

Minuchin, S., 2, 54
mood disorder, 26, 69

neurobiological research, 2, 10, 57, 74
Norcross, J., 27

Oaklander, V., 75, 104, 155
O'Connor, K., 8, 14
O'Donohue, J., 106

Play Therapy Decision Grid, 4–5
puppet play, 59, 68, 75, 92, 102, 104

"quest for home" strategies, 131–144

relational questions, 24, 59, 136
relational domains, 4, 6, 7, 9, 12–13, 15, 17–19, 21–23, 25–29, 31, 33, 35–36, 37, 39–40, 42, 55, 59, 95, 117, 119, 136, 143
relational strategies, 7–28, 117
relational therapy, 2, 4, 29
relational theory, 2, 4, 6, 18, 22, 27, 29, 35–36, 42, 55, 59, 136, 143
resilience, 53, 57, 114, 155–57
resistance, 22, 27, 29

sand play, 30, 32
Sarnoff, C. A., 85
Schore, A., 2, 9
secrets, family, 135–37
self-observer, 57–82
shame, 2, 19, 60, 80, 94, 96, 113–14, 140–42
sibling rivalry, 60, 62
Siegel, D., 2, 10, 57, 82
Silverstein, O., iii, 66
social rejection, 38, 72, 99–115
sorrow, 82, 126, 157
stigma 2–3, 94, 113–14, 140
storytelling: storytelling, references, 160; strengths-based approach, 45–55; therapy stories for adolescents, 65–66, 79, 81, 108–111, 140–143;

therapy stories for children, 51,
59–60, 63, 65–66, 69–70, 79, 88,
100–101, 120, 122, 131, 148, 153;
therapeutic use of storytelling, 2–4,
6, 114
symbol work: symbol work with the
heart shape, 9, 13, 17, 21–22. 25–26;
symbol work with loss, 118–19, 127,
129–30, 133, 135, 137, 139; symbols,
references, 159–61,163–64; symbol
work with strengths, 46, 53, 150,
153, 155–56; symbol work with
stories, 46, 52, 63, 68–69, 70, 75, 80,
90, 104, 142; symbol work in
supervision, 26; symbol work with
words, evocative, 29–43; therapeutic
use of symbols, 3–4, 9, 13, 42, 130
symbolic play: therapeutic use of play,
2–5, 8, 16, 30, 32, 37, 59 94; directive
play scenarios, 62, 68, 70, 75, 83–86,
92, 99, 102, 104; play therapy,
references, 160–65

Tangney, J. P., 60, 96
terror, 19, 79, 129
therapeutic strategies: Alligator in the
Swamp, 83–86; Animal that No One
wants to Hug, 86–93; ; Ballistic
Stallion, 145–50; Behind Closed
Doors, 108–14; Blow-Up Bernie,
63–69; Boy who Sit alone in the
Cafeteria, 105–08; Bumblebee who
Stings Everyone, 99–105; Bunny is
Lost, 131–33; Empathy for Others
and Self, 95–96; Heartfelt Feelings
Coloring Card Strategies (HFCCS),
17–28; Heartfelt Feelings Strategies
(HFS), 7–17; Hellos and Good-byes,
117–19; Homes on the

Inside/Outside, 135–37; ; House of
Hopes, Dreams, and Promises,
137–140; Linking Object, 126–30;
Magic Key, 124–126; Magic Stones,
150–51; Mike's Version of Russian
Roulette, 75–80; Misunderstood
Mouse, 69–73; Patsy Anne, 50–52;
Pig that didn't Fit, 119–24; Puppy in
the Animal Shelter, 133–35; Secret
Life of Nicole, 140–143; Standing
Ovation, 52–53; Symbol Association
Therapy Strategies (SATS), 29–43;
Tree on the top of the Hill, 152–53;
Unsung Heroes and Heroines,
45–52; Wise Ole Owl Speaks,
57–63
trauma: expressed in play, 86; family
trauma, 40, 95; finding meaning and
purpose, 57; neurobiology of trauma,
38, 80; relationship trauma, 36;
traumatized children, 5, 8, 72,
74–75, 153; traumatic grief,
117–130; trauma, references, 161–63,
165

violence: violence of children, 60, 74–75,
81, 97; violence, domestic, 68, 97,
126, 135; violence, exposure to, 66,
72, 74, 153; violence, potential for,
93, 108, 144; violence, references,
162, 164
Volkan, V. D., 126

Waters, D. B., 54
White, R., 54
wisdom, 10, 58–59, 108
Worden, J. W., 127

Zahn-Waxler, C., 94

261078BV00004B/1/P